FETCH!

A HOW TO SPEAK DOG TRAINING GUIDE

AUBRE ANDRUS &

GARY WEITZMAN, D.V.M.,
PRESIDENT & CEO OF THE SAN DIEGO
HUMANE SOCIETY

NATIONAL GEOGRAPHIC
WASHINGTON, D.C.

CONTENTS

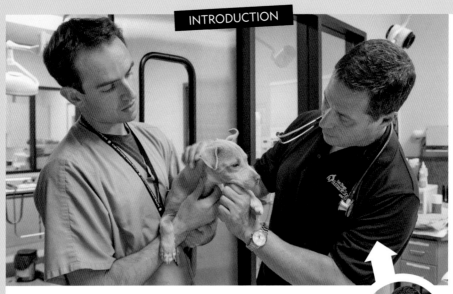

Meet **Dr.Gary**

Veterinarian and Dog Expert

 Your dog is listening to you! Did you know that dogs can understand about 150 words and gestures like "sit," "fetch," and "roll over"? In fact, they have nearly the same level of word understanding as a two-year-old human! Amazing, right? But your pup wasn't born with the ability to perform tricks. It takes a lot of time, practice, and understanding from both the owner and the pet. Are you up for the challenge?

My name is Dr. Gary Weitzman, and I'll be your guide through this book. I'm a veterinarian and the president of the San Diego Humane Society in California, U.S.A. For more than 30 years, I've observed the relationships between thousands of dogs and their owners. If I've learned one thing, it is that with hard work dogs and their owners can communicate with each other.

Throughout these pages, I'll share tips and training strategies so that you can teach your dog new skills. You'll learn why some pups are easier to train than others, what commands are best for your pet, and so much more. Every dog is different—just like every human is different. You might be good at kicking a soccer ball into a goal, while your friend might excel at playing the piano. We all have unique skill levels, likes and dislikes, as well as talents. And our pets do too!

With this book, you'll understand how dogs best learn. We'll cover everything from how often you should practice, to what you should say, to how you can reward good behavior. You'll also discover why playing with your dog is important. We've even included instructions for a few dog toys and treats you can make yourself.

So keep reading. There's so much for you and your dog to discover. Now it's time for you and your furry friend to emBARK on this adventure together!

A NOTE TO **PARENTS**

The activities in this book are designed to be fun for both kids and their pets. Just like humans, dogs enjoy new challenges! For safety purposes, we recommend that your young dog trainer have adult supervision for ALL of the activities in this book. Before your child begins an activity, please read and discuss the following dog SAFETY GUIDELINES with your child, to make sure that both your child and your dog are safe, comfortable, and having fun. Only do these activities with your own pet.

DOG SAFETY

- Remember that dogs, like all animals, can be unpredictable.
- Only do these activities with your dog if he knows your child well and is comfortable around your child.
- Watch for signs that your dog is unhappy. If any of these activities seem to make him uncomfortable or upset, stop immediately.
- Even a dog that is enjoying an activity needs a break. Make sure your dog has access to water throughout these activities, and if he wants to stop, let him.
- If your dog is on a special diet, check

with his veterinarian before feeding him treats. Tell your child always to check with an adult before feeding your dog anything.
- Clean up when you are done so your canine pal doesn't accidentally eat any leftover materials.
- If you decide to alter an activity or try a new version, make sure the new plan is safe for both your child and the dog.

FOR YOUR **SAFETY**

We have made sure that the training tips, scenarios, and interpretations of dog behavior in this book come from the most accurate and up-to-date sources.

Much of the advice and guidance in this book requires close observation of dogs, but even so there may be behavior that the observer (you!) can miss. That means we always need to be cautious with dogs—those that are strangers to you and your own pets.

If you are following the steps from this book and your dog seems upset, stop what you are doing and approach it in a new way, or try again later.

SIT

ROLL OVER

HEEL

8

Why **TRAIN** Your Dog?

Giving your dog a high five is cool! But "being cool" is just one of the many reasons to train your pet. After all, training is about a lot more than teaching a pup fun tricks. A well-trained dog is often a well-behaved dog. When a pet can follow the rules—and knows when to stop barking or jumping up—she'll fit in better with your family and your home. That means life can run more smoothly for everyone.

A well-behaved dog can also mean a safe dog. Teaching your canine how to go on a proper walk is important. When a dog can understand "Heel" or "Sit," you can help keep her away from oncoming traffic. And you can say "Drop it" if she picks up something unsafe in her mouth while you are at the park. It's easy to see how these "tricks" can become so important to a dog's health and safety.

Training is also a great way to bond with your pet. Teaching a new skill takes a lot of time and practice, and by doing it, you'll learn how to communicate better with each other. You'll also gain trust and respect—especially when you reward good behavior. And training will give you and your dog the confidence needed to be the best partners imaginable.

Humans and dogs need exercise for both their bodies and their brains. Learning from and inter-acting with people are just as important as running around the backyard. A long walk, where you practice skills along the way, is the perfect way for you and your pet to get exercise, to train, and to bond. Grab your leash—let's go!

Learning from and interacting with people are just as important as running around the backyard.

UNDERSTANDING
Your Dog

WHEN YOU UNDERSTAND how your dog communicates, listens, learns, and explores the world, you can better train your dog.

TAIL

Your dog's tail can have up to **23 vertebrae, or small bones,** depending on his breed. This series of bumpy bones keeps his tail flexible, which means he can move it in all different directions. His tail movement is important because a dog uses his tail for balance, somewhat like a counterweight.

LEGS

You'll find the **most powerful muscles** in a dog's body are in his hind legs. A dog's elbow is close to his body, and what looks like a backward knee is actually his back ankle. In the same way humans are left- or right-handed, dogs have a dominant limb too.

CEREBRUM

When you say "Fetch!" your dog's cerebrum, a part of his brain, is hard at work. His ears take in that information and then send it there for processing. The cerebrum helps him **learn, remember, and make decisions.** Soon, his brain will tell his legs to get moving.

CEREBELLUM

When your dog runs to fetch a ball, he's able to move each leg in coordination with the others, as well as open his mouth at just the right time to grab the ball. The cerebellum, another part of his brain, is **responsible for balance** and helps a dog's muscles move in just the right way.

EARS

Whether dogs' ears are long and floppy or short and pricked, they **can hear much better than humans.** Pups with short, pricked ears can move their ears, which means they take in more sound waves than we can. And all dogs' ear canals are deeper than humans', which allows sound to carry better to their eardrums.

EYES

Dogs are very **good at seeing movement,** but they aren't so great at seeing color. They see color differently than us, and they see fewer colors. Everything looks yellow, blue, or gray (even if it's not!). It is very difficult for dogs to see the color red.

NOSE

Experts say your pooch's sense of smell is at least 10,000 times better than yours. That means dogs can smell things long before humans can, and they can sniff out things we don't notice at all. This is partly because dogs have two big nostrils with slits along the sides. Dogs breathe in through their nostrils and out through the slits, so they take in and **experience smells for a longer period of time** than we can.

TONGUE

Dogs have taste buds just like humans do, but they have a lot fewer. We have about 9,000, and they have only 1,700. But most pups gobble their food so quickly that they can barely taste it. Even so, they still love to be rewarded with treats!

HISTORY
of Training

THROUGHOUT HISTORY, humans have bred different kinds of dogs together to make pups smarter and stronger. New breeds were created with specific talents or characteristics that could help people. Thanks to their unique physical or mental qualities, these breeds can be trained to do amazing things like guard the streets or herd sheep.

1500s

BEAGLES were bred to work in packs and have been used to hunt rabbits and track deer in England since the 1500s. This dog breed has a very keen sense of smell and a strong hunting instinct.

1600s

STANDARD POODLES were originally bred as duck hunters and have excelled at swimming and retrieving for more than 400 years. They are especially athletic and intelligent.

1700s

BORDER COLLIES were bred to herd livestock and are famous for being able to round up sheep and get them in a pen. They love having a job to do and are known for their laser-sharp focus.

1800s

DALMATIANS have a protective instinct because they were originally bred to act as guard dogs that trotted alongside horse-drawn carriages. When some of those horse-drawn carriages became fire engines, the Dalmatians accompanying them became associated with firefighters.

LATE 1800s /EARLY 1900s

GERMAN SHEPHERDS are loyal dogs that are known to be courageous and willing to defend their human companions. This breed often trains and serves with the police and military.

Can You **TEACH** an Old Dog New Tricks?

A popular saying is "You can't teach an old dog new tricks." It means that once someone is older you can't change their habits or behavior and they can't learn a new skill. But it turns out the saying is not true—for humans or for dogs!

Although it is ideal to train a puppy, an older dog can learn new skills and tricks. It simply may take longer than it would to teach a puppy—possibly more than twice as long. But studies have found that the dog will eventually learn the skill and be able to perform and remember it in the same way a younger dog could.

Remember that older dogs may have less physical ability than younger dogs. They may not be able to run fast or jump if they have joint pain. They also may have some hearing or vision issues that prevent them from learning certain things.

Talk to your veterinarian about your older dog's health and abilities before you begin training.

It's true that older dogs or rescue dogs whose previous owners didn't train them may have some bad habits, but they can change their ways. Peeing in the house, chewing everything, or barking at strangers can be corrected with practice. It helps to understand why the dog is acting that way in the first place.

If you have a rescue dog, good for you! Give her time to adjust to your new home. She has to learn that she is loved and safe. Once you begin training, assume that she has no previous training experience. Start from the very beginning. It may take some extra patience, but these "underdogs" can learn good behavior and some new tricks.

While it is ideal to **train a puppy,** an older dog can learn new tricks.

Daily practice is part of the training process.

When **CAN** I Start Training?

If you have the chance, the best time to start training a dog is when she is a puppy. Puppies are born deaf and blind and need to stay with their mothers until they are at least eight weeks old. They can begin potty training immediately, but basic commands are best taught after eight weeks of age, which is when they are usually adopted. If you delay training too long, they may learn bad habits.

Puppies have short attention spans, meaning they can only focus for brief amounts of time. This is why they likely will not understand basic commands until they are about eight weeks old. But daily practice is part of the training process. In fact, all basic commands should be practiced and reinforced every day for the first year of a puppy's life.

An ideal plan is to work with your dog for at least 15 minutes a day. If it seems better for you and your dog, this can be broken up into five-minute sessions. Remember that puppies grow a lot in their first year and their bones and joints aren't fully formed. This means puppies need a lot of time to rest too. Ask your veterinarian how much exercise is just right for your dog's breed, size, and age, as well as when it's safe for her to socialize and venture out into the world. While at the vet, be sure also to have your parents ask which shots your dog needs to help her immune system grow strong and to keep her healthy.

THE FIRST FEW **SKILLS**

Puppies aged eight weeks and up can start learning the following commands.

SIT
page 44

STAY
page 46

DOWN
page 48

STAND
page 50

Is My Dog **READY** to Be Trained?

USE THIS CHART as a guide to see if your dog might be ready for training.

START

Is your dog at least **EIGHT WEEKS** old?

YES

What kind of dog do you have?

NO

Your puppy is not yet ready to learn basic commands.

An older dog or a rescue dog

Awesome! Before you begin, talk to your veterinarian about your dog's physical abilities and health.

A puppy

That's great! This is the perfect time to start training your pup.

Have you read the **Before You Begin** section on pages 20–39?

YES

Perfect. Consistency is important when it comes to learning a new skill. It's great that you're ready to commit lots of time to training your dog! Let's get started. Turn to page 40 to begin your first skill.

YES

Cool. Are you able to practice this skill a few more times today, as well as every day for the rest of the week?

YES

Fantastic! Let's get started. Are you standing in a space that's free from distractions (such as a quiet place in your backyard)?

NO

Maybe this isn't a great time to introduce a new skill to your dog. Wait until you have time to practice consistently with your pup.

NO

Move to a space with fewer people and less noise so your dog can better concentrate. You want your pup to be successful!

NO

Start reading! Before you can teach your dog a command, you'll need to learn the basics of how dogs learn.

BEFORE YOU BEGIN

YOU'VE PROBABLY SEEN a dog owner say "Sit" and watched the dog quickly follow the command. Easy, right? Not exactly. There is a science behind training. Once you begin to understand it, you'll be better set for success in your new role: dog trainer extraordinaire!

In this chapter, we'll cover certain rules and tips that will help make the training process more fun for you and your dog. You'll discover how a dog learns—it's a little bit different than how you learn. Cues, rewards, and reinforcement are tools that you'll use to teach your pup new skills. By offering signs, or cues, your dog will begin to understand what you're asking him to do. When he does it correctly, you'll give him a reward so he wants to do it again. And by repeating the same steps of each skill over and over, you will strengthen, or reinforce, his good behavior.

We'll also consider some of the characteristics of your specific dog. His physical characteristics as well as his person-ality can affect how and what he learns, and how fast he learns it. You are also an important part of the equation. How often you can commit to practicing and how long you can consistently train with your dog will make a big difference.

DON'T SKIP OVER THIS CHAPTER—it's the foundation for all the skills the two of you will tackle later in the book. And it's the basis for all dog training. Using this knowledge, you could teach your pup to do dozens of skills!

There's **NO PUP** Like Yours

Like Snowflakes, Every Dog Is Different

How well do you know your dog? If you've just become the proud owner of a new puppy, take some time to observe your furry friend. Personality traits or characteristics, like whether he is playful or shy, or prefers sprinting or sniffing the sidewalk, will become clear the longer you spend time together.

Keep this in mind: Some dogs will be easier to train than others. There are so many factors! Your veterinarian can help answer any questions or concerns you have about your pet's abilities.

What Breed Is Your Dog?

Certain breeds—like border collies, German shepherds, poodles, golden retrievers, and Labrador retrievers— are better at learning than others. If you don't know what breed your dog is, or if he is a mix, that's OK. This is just one clue into helping you understand your dog's abilities to concentrate and learn.

What Is His Body Size and Shape?

Dogs have physical limitations just like humans do. For example, someone who is six feet (1.8 m) tall may be better at making a slam dunk than someone who is five feet (1.5 m) tall. Keep in mind whether your pooch is short, tall, big, small, strong, frail, light, or heavy.

How Old Is He?

Older dogs can learn new skills and tricks, but they might take longer to pick up on new ones. Puppies might learn faster, but they often get tired quickly. Both puppies and older dogs could have weaker muscles or bones that keep them from jumping high or running far.

What Is His Personality?

You know your dog best. Maybe he has a short attention span and needs to play and burn off some energy before he trains. Or maybe he is very patient and loves to learn. Keep this in mind during training, and tailor your session to your dog's abilities.

⚠ SAFETY FIRST

EVEN WITH a lot of practice and patience, your pup might not be able to learn a certain skill. It's OK! Don't force your pet to do something he doesn't want to do. Never hit your dog or jerk his collar.

DECODE Your Dog

Actions Speak Louder Than Barks

Animals can't speak English, Arabic, or any other language that people speak. But they do communicate another way—through the movements of their body. It's called body language! The placement of their ears, tail, and even their tongue can help tell you how they are feeling. If you know the signs, you'll be able to better understand when your dog is interested in learning a new skill or if she's afraid.

DR. GARY'S **TRAINING TIPS**

Calm an anxious pup with a good run. When dogs run, they release endorphins, which are feel-good chemicals that can help them feel less stressed. Going for a fast walk or a run will help you release endorphins too. Dogs can pick up on their owners' emotions, so when you relax, your dog does too. It's a win-win!

Good Signs

These gestures indicate that it is a good time to teach a new command or practice one you've already learned. They show your dog is feeling friendly and ready to train:

- Loose, wiggly body
- Lying belly-up
- Tongue hanging loosely from mouth
- Fast, wagging tail (large sweeping motion)
- Ears in a neutral, relaxed position
- Tail in a neutral, relaxed position
- Straight tail, raised level with back
- Stutter bark (sounds like arrr-RUFF)

Bad Signs

Take a break from training and try again another time when you see your dog do any of the following, as she may be feeling nervous, stressed, or anxious:

- Stiff, tight body
- Freezing in place
- Erect ears
- Teeth bared
- Low tail or stiff, high tail
- Tail tucked low between legs
- Growling
- Panting

IF A DOG GROWLS, bares her teeth, and freezes in place, she is likely angry and may attack. Always keep your safety in mind and step far away from any animal that seems angry.

Dog
BEHAVIOR

 Dogs are born with natural behaviors, just like animals that live in the wild. Learning what might drive a dog to act a certain way can help you better understand your pup's thinking—and give you a little more patience during training.

Dogs crave attention, but they get distracted.

Your pup is a playful creature that loves attention, especially from you. But whatever is the most exciting thing in the room will call her attention away. Don't be surprised if you lose her attention while teaching a skill because—squirrel!

Dogs learn differently.

Dogs can memorize many commands, but "right" and "wrong" don't come so easily to them. They need practice to remember something new.

Dogs like rewards.

When it comes to dogs—and people!—behaviors that are rewarded will be repeated more often. And behaviors that are not rewarded will be repeated less often. You'll need a stash of small and healthy treats if you want to train your dog.

Dogs have a history.

Your behaviors, habits, and skills depend on your experiences and background. The same can be said for your dog. All dogs have learned certain behaviors—some good and some that need correcting—and will take time to change.

How Dogs LEARN

Let's say your family makes up a new rule like, "Make your bed every morning before school." It is possible for you to remember this new rule by being told about it just one time. But dogs can't do that.

Dogs learn slowly by hearing a command, performing an action, and then being rewarded for that action. A cue is a signal for your dog to do something for you. It can be a verbal request like "Sit" or a hand gesture. Think of it like a firm request to tell your pet what to do. After some time, the dog will realize that a specific cue demands a particular behavior, which gets a certain response from you—hopefully a good one!

Voice Commands

Voice commands are one kind of cue that prompts your pup to act a certain way. Dogs can learn more than 100 words and gestures. In this book, we'll introduce about 30 of them.

Hand Signals

Because dogs express themselves through body language, you could try pairing a hand signal with a voice command. Together, your hand and voice become a cue. With practice, your pup may be able to react when she sees a gesture, even without hearing you say anything. This can be helpful for elderly dogs that are hard of hearing.

Reinforcement

Reinforcement is when you offer a consequence, like a treat or a pat on the back, after your dog follows your instructions. Offering your dog a reinforcement helps increase the chance that the behavior will happen again. In this book, we'll cover how to use positive reinforcement to teach your pup new skills. It's important to give positive reinforcement, meaning kind and good consequences, every time your dog follows your cues.

Marker Training

Clickers, which are mechanical noise-makers, and marker words, or verbal commands, can be helpful during a training session because they high-light the exact action that will be rewarded. With a bit of practice, a dog can learn that a clicking noise or a certain word means "Good job! A treat is on the way!"

TREATS for Tricks

 Let's say your cousins are visiting next week and you are told to clean your room before they arrive. Wouldn't you be more likely to make your room sparkling clean if you were given money as a reward? Most likely, yes.

Your pup feels the same way. Let's say you want to teach him how to sit. You have two options: You could reward him when he does it correctly, or you could punish him when he does it incorrectly. When it comes to dog training, it's best to use positive reinforcement.

When your dog hears the command "Sit," and then takes a seat on the ground, you "pay" him with a treat. That's positive reinforcement, just like the $5 you'd earn for cleaning your room. Positive reinforcement teaches your dog that if he follows your cue, he'll get a reward. The goal is to increase, or reinforce, the behavior with the addition of something good—the treat.

Behavioral scientists study actions and mannerisms. They try to understand why humans or animals act the way they do. These behavioral scientists found that positive reinforcement is the best way to teach your dog. Punishing your dog for incorrect behaviors could make your furry friend anxious or fearful of you. That's the exact opposite of what you're trying to do! Training is about building a good relationship with your dog and creating a sense of trust.

DR. GARY'S **TRAINING TIPS**

Treats should be small so they are easy to eat quickly. Good training treats include small pieces of a dog biscuit or cut-up hot dog. Make sure you hand the treat directly to your dog instead of making him walk to a treat that's been thrown on the floor. Don't overtreat your pup! Too many treats can lead to an unhealthy pet, and they can devalue the treat.

When it comes to **dog training,** it's best to use **positive** reinforcement.

DOES YOUR PUP **NEED A TREAT** EVERY TIME?

In the first few weeks of training, dogs need consistency and predictability. So they'll need a reward every time they complete a trick. But once a behavior is learned, a treat is no longer necessary. Eventually, with enough practice, the hope is that you will be able to get your pet to sit regardless of whether or not you have a treat hiding in your hand. However, an occasional reinforcement with a treat is nice.

To a dog, any valued item is a reward. This could be a tasty treat, a toy, a play session with you, a "good boy," or even a pat on the head. Keep that in mind as the two of you work together. Pay attention to what reward makes him especially happy and excited so you can use it again and again.

TRAINING TREATS

Here are some regular treats you can use on a daily basis when you start out training:

- small pieces of a dog biscuit
- cut-up hot dog
- small pieces from a dog food roll*

The following are considered high-value treats that should be saved for more difficult training sessions, like trying to keep a dog's attention when a squirrel is nearby:

- sardines
- cat food
- rawhide
- small pieces of string cheese

* You can also look for a squeezable dog training food tube online and fill it yourself with pureed dog food. One portion will be squeezed directly into your dog's mouth.

DO I NEED A **CLICKER?**

No! You don't need a clicker. Studies have found that speaking a marker word works just as well as pressing a clicker. Try saying a word like "yes" or "good" to mark an action. You could even say the word "click" if you really want to!

First you'll need to train your dog that the marker word will earn him a treat. This can be done by reciting the word, and then immediately giving your dog a treat. Repeat this 10 to 20 times.

CLICK, CLICK,
That's the Trick!

A dolphin trainer blows a whistle just as the dolphin leaps into the air. "Yes!" the dolphin thinks. "I get a treat because I jumped extra high!" Marine mammal trainers developed this kind of positive reinforcement training to help dolphins understand exactly which part of a trick was earning a reward.

When a whistle marks a precise moment during a trick, the dolphin can better understand what the trainer was looking for—and how to earn his next treat. Was it the big splash or the high jump? The whistle helps clear up any confusion.

While marine trainers use whistles, which can be heard underwater, dog trainers prefer clickers. A dog training clicker is a tiny handheld device that makes a clicking noise when it's pressed. They are inexpensive and can be found online or at pet stores. They often hang from a key ring that can be attached to a leash or an elastic bracelet.

How to Use a Dog Training Clicker

Before you get started, you have to teach your dog that a click means "a treat is on its way!" This is called "charging" the clicker. (You can break this into two different training sessions.) To do this, you'll need 10 to 20 small treats. Click just before you feed your dog each treat. One click equals one treat. Make sure to feed the treats within three seconds of the click.

❶ Cue your dog to perform a skill. Find ideas starting on page 40. Start with the simplest skills first.

❷ Mark the skill. Press the clicker to mark the exact moment that matters. It's the moment he's completing the action. For example, if you're teaching your dog to sit, click the clicker the moment his bottom hits the floor.

❸ Reward success! That way he can associate the clicking noise with the reward and know that performing the trick will earn him a treat.

How **MARKER TRAINING** Works

In the late 1800s and early 1900s, a Russian scientist named Ivan Pavlov conducted a series of experiments on dogs. During those experiments, the dogs needed to be fed. Scientists in white lab coats would bring the food.

Pavlov knew that when dogs eat, they drool. It's an unconditioned response, which means it's a natural response that the dogs don't even think about. It just happens! But Pavlov noticed something interesting: The pups began drooling whenever a scientist in a white lab coat appeared ... before they even saw the food!

BELL EXPERIMENT

If you rang a bell in front of your pet, nothing would happen. But if you rang a bell every time you poured more food into his bowl, he would soon learn that a ringing bell equals food. Before long, your dog would come running to his food bowl every time you rang the bell. Cool, huh?

The dogs had learned to salivate in response to something associated with the food instead of just for the food itself. This is called classical conditioning. Classical conditioning lets you teach a dog to associate one thing with another—specifically, an automatic response (like drooling) with something that's unrelated (like a white lab coat).

But the responses don't have to be automatic. You can teach your dog that one behavior leads to another. This process is called operant conditioning. Your dog understands that a certain learned behavior can produce a certain consequence.

So what do all these big conditioning words and phrases mean? To say it simply: Following a command can bring a yummy reward.

Animal trainers use the findings from Pavlov's experiment in clicker training. When the dogs hear a click, they get a treat. The click is associated with a reward. If you click only when your dog performs a command correctly, he'll learn that a click means "Good job!"

You can **teach** your dog that one behavior can **lead** to another.

DR. GARY'S **TRAINING TIPS**

Your dog can memorize a command in any language—it doesn't have to be in English. In Spanish, "Sit" is *Siéntate*; in Chinese, it's *Zuo xia*; and in pig Latin, it's *It-say!*

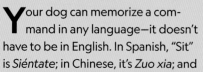

Your Dog Is **LISTENING!**

Training requires a lot of communication with your dog. Not only do you have to speak a specific word, but you also have to speak it in the same tone of voice.

What You Say

Dogs can learn words for commands, but only when you use them consistently. It's important that everyone in your family use the exact same word for the exact same command every time.

For example, "Down" is a command that could mean either "Don't jump on me" or "Lie down on the floor." Do you see how that could be confusing for your dog? Instead, use two commands. Say "Off" when you want the dog to get off of you or another object and "Down" when you want him to lie on the floor.

It's also best if commands are only one word. Keep them as short and simple as possible. "Down" is better than "Lie down," and "Come" is better than "Come here." Don't expect your dog to understand different versions of the same phrase. He doesn't know that "Come over here now!" means the same thing as "Come."

In this book, we've already chosen words for commands that are short and specific. You don't have to use these words. But we offer them to you to make it easier for you and your dog to remember and repeat.

How You Say It

Have you ever walked up to a baby and started talking to her in a high-pitched voice? We naturally tend to do this for both babies and dogs. Funny, right? But that intuition can be helpful during training. When you teach a command like "Stay," you probably automatically slow your voice down and speak in a low, steady tone. It might sound like this: "Staaaaaaaaay." Speaking in a long, slow manner helps calm an animal. They'll be more likely to relax and be better able to perform a simple command.

The opposite is true for when you want your pet to spring into action-hero mode. Short, rapidly repeated sounds work great for active commands like "Come" or "Jump." Whether you're speaking fast or slow, loud or soft, it's important to remain relaxed during a training session. Dogs can pick up on your emotions. A calm trainer will get better results.

Practice Makes
PERFECT

Dog training takes time—about 15 minutes a day is best. You'll want to focus on one command in each session. Don't overwhelm your dog and try to teach her 10 different skills in one day. Master one skill before moving on to the next one. Even after she's got it, keep practicing each learned command so she doesn't forget.

How Long Will It Take?

It's hard to say how quickly a dog will learn to perform and remember a new skill. Dog behavior specialists recommend that a new puppy be trained every day for a full year. It's a big time commitment.

Be sure to keep each training session short. The 15-minute daily requirement can be broken into three five-minute sessions, especially if your dog seems frustrated or tired. Try to end on a positive note with a cuddle session or with a skill she's already mastered and loves. Remember: This should be fun for both of you.

What's Considered a Success?

Your dog performed a command. Hooray! But it was only that one time.

Shoot! We didn't say it would be easy. Dogs need practice just like you do. You can pat yourself on the back if your pup can correctly perform the skill five times in a row. If your dog doesn't get five out of five, try another set of five. Keep score of how well she performs. She'll improve little by little.

Once you feel comfortable as a team, try practicing in different places like the backyard or at a park. You want your dog to be able to respond to your commands anywhere and everywhere, not just in your living room. Very slowly introduce distractions like other people or a new environment. Of course, if you do head to a park, be sure to grab a grown-up and make sure the rules allow for your dog to be off her leash.

What if My Dog Doesn't Listen?

When your dog doesn't perform a command, it's important that you do not give the reward. Not giving a reward is called "canceling" a treat. You might even want to walk away, give your dog a short break, or stop training for the day.

Dogs need **practice**
just like **you do.**

BASIC TRAINING

E VERY DOG—BIG OR SMALL—can benefit from learning the basic commands featured in this chapter. When you bring a dog or puppy into your home, these are the first lessons you should try to teach. (Remember, even an older pet can learn new skills!)

These skills will help your pup behave better at home on a daily basis. They'll help you communicate to your dog what's allowed and what's not. And most important, they'll help the two of you establish a healthy relationship.

Although all of the commands in this chapter are important, remember that training takes time. You learned the alphabet before you learned how to read, right? When it comes to dog training, it helps to follow similar advice. It's best to start at the beginning of this chapter and teach the commands from this chapter in order. Each skill builds on the one before it.

YOU NEED

▶ A quiet space free from distractions so you and your dog can focus

▶ An attentive dog (observe the signs of a happy dog on page 24)

▶ About 15 minutes a day (can be spaced out in three five-minute sessions)

▶ Small and healthy treats for a reward

▶ Optional: a clicker

COME

 Every dog should learn his own name and to come when called. Eventually, you'd like your dog to run up to you the first time you call for him. It's possible! For this command, use your pup's name followed by the word "come." For example, "Fido, come."

It's important first to practice with your pet on a leash, so he has no other choice but to come to you.

INSTRUCTIONS

1. Start with your dog a short distance away from you on a leash.
2. Begin jogging and give a gentle tug on the leash so he follows you as you say "Fido, come." Don't repeat the command over and over. Once is enough.
3. When he follows, stop and reward him with a treat. Repeat this process five times.
4. Now hold a treat in your hand while your dog is a short distance away from you on the leash.
5. Say "Fido, come." Reward him with the treat when he comes to you. Repeat five times.

Once you've mastered "Come" on the leash, you can try this command off the leash in your own home.

DR. GARY'S TRAINING TIPS

When you first begin teaching this skill, only call your dog when you know he's likely to come (like when you're running and he will want to join you or when you're holding a treat and he can see it). Reward him every time. If your dog still won't come when called, turn to page 132 to review how to correct some common mistakes you might be making, so your dog will learn the command better.

SIT

The "Sit" command is especially helpful for dogs that like to jump up on people or couches. One way to help stop bad behavior is by rewarding good behavior. This command gives your pet something better to do—"Sit! Good dog!"

INSTRUCTIONS

1. Hold a treat near her nose. Slowly lift the treat above her head and back toward her tail, which will encourage her to lower her rear end.
2. As soon as she begins to bend her knees and her bottom hits the floor, reward her with a treat. Only give a reward when she's in the sitting position.
3. Repeat five times.
4. When your dog begins to master this skill, add the cue "Sit" as you perform the skill together. Once she's mastered it, she should be able to sit with the verbal cue only.

DR. GARY'S **TRAINING TIPS**

Don't push your dog into a sitting position. It won't help her learn more quickly. You want your dog to move her muscles on her own. Once she's got this skill down, increase the amount of time she must stay sitting before she's given her reward. This will help her understand that you may need her to sit for more than just a few seconds (for example, at the curb of a sidewalk before you cross the street).

OPTIONAL: **HAND GESTURE**

Start with your arm hanging at the side of your body with your palm facing out. Bend your elbow and raise your forearm toward your shoulder as you say "Sit."

STAY

Once your dog has learned how to sit, you can teach him how to stay. These two cues are a great setup for more advanced skills later in the book because they allow your dog to pause, focus, and listen for the next command.

Teach a Release Word

When you teach him how to stay, you'll have to teach him a release word that cues him that it's OK to start moving again. We'll use the word "OK."

INSTRUCTIONS

1. Cue your dog to "Sit" (page 44) and then reward him.
2. Now, encourage your dog to move by jogging away from him or enticing him with a treat or toy. As you do this say "OK."
3. Reward him with a treat when he begins to move.
4. Repeat five times.

DR. GARY'S **TRAINING TIPS**

Keep practicing this skill, but slowly make it more difficult by taking a step away from your pup. Eventually, you can take more and more steps away from your pup, turn your back on him, or even walk into the next room.

46

DOWN

This may be one of the commands you use most. Let's face it—sometimes dogs need a little help calming down. In this case, "Down" means "Lie down"—not "Off" like "Get off of me." For help with a dog who likes to jump up on people, turn to page 124 for training advice.

INSTRUCTIONS

1 Cue your dog into a "Sit" position (page 44) and reward her with a treat.

2 Hold a second treat in front of her nose. Very slowly bring the treat down to the floor between her front paws.

3 If your dog's nose followed the treat all the way to the floor, reward her with a treat. If she stands, take away the treat and start over. Reward her only when she gets into and stays in the "Down" position.

4 Repeat five times.

5 When your dog begins to master this skill, add the cue "Down" as you perform the skill together. At first, try saying it as she is actively moving from the sitting to lying position. When she understands what the cue means, say it just before she begins to lie down from the sitting position. Once she's mastered the skill, she should be able to perform it with the verbal cue only.

DR. GARY'S **TRAINING TIPS**

Like "Stay" (page 46), this command can use a release word like "OK" (page 46) to let your dog know when it's appropriate to get up and start moving.

 OPTIONAL: **HAND GESTURE**

Bend your elbow with your open palm facing downward, like you're about to dribble a basketball. Move your palm slowly toward the ground as you say "Down."

STAND

You probably won't cue your dog to stand as much as you will ask her to sit or lie down. But standing on command can be helpful for tasks like grooming and bathing. Remember that standing for a dog means four legs are on the ground—not two!

INSTRUCTIONS

❶ Cue your dog to "Sit" (page 44).

❷ Hold a treat in front of your dog's nose.

❸ Pull the treat slowly toward you (straight out from the dog's nose).

❹ The moment she lifts her rear end to follow the treat, say "Good." Reward her with a treat.

❺ Repeat five times.

❻ When your dog begins to master this skill, add the cue "Stand" as you perform the skill together. Once she's mastered the skill, she should be able to perform it with the verbal cue only.

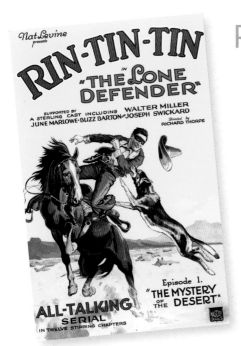

Rin-Tin-Tin was a very famous **German shepherd** that **acted** in dozens of movies. He was even **nominated** for an Academy Award!

 OPTIONAL: **HAND GESTURE**

Hang your arm loosely at your side with your palm facing outward. Then slowly move your arm backward as you say "Stand."

NO

 Dogs are naturally curious. They also love to put things in their mouths. Unfortunately, they don't always know whether something is harmful to them or when their behavior is not OK. The "No" command can help your dog avoid dangerous objects outside or in the house and can help teach her right from wrong.

INSTRUCTIONS

1 Place a handful of treats in your closed fist. Place a secret stash of treats somewhere within reach so you can quickly reward your dog.

2 Present your closed fist to your dog. She will try to sniff the treats out of your hand. When she stops, say "Good" and reward her with a treat from the secret nearby stash—not from your closed fist.

3 Repeat five times. Begin saying "No" at the moment when you present your fist.

4 Now slightly open your closed fist with the treats and say "No." If she tries to grab the treats, close your fist and try again. If she leaves the treats, say "Good" and reward her with a treat from your secret stash. Repeat step 4 at least five times.

5 Now place the treats on the floor with your hand cupped over them. Say "No." If she leaves the treats, say "Good" and reward her with a treat from your secret stash. Repeat step 5 at least five times.

6 Place the treats on the floor without your hand cupped over them. Remove your hand and say "No." If she leaves the treats, say "Good" and reward her with a treat from your secret stash. Repeat this step at least five times.

DR. GARY'S **TRAINING TIPS**

This skill might have to be taught over multiple training sessions as you increase the level of difficulty. Each step is a level of difficulty that your dog should master before moving on to the next.

WAIT

"Wait" is different from "Stay" (page 46) in that you're asking your dog to take a short pause for just a few seconds before you release him. And it's different from "Place" (coming up on page 106) because you want to use this cue whether you're at home or away.

Learning how to wait is a good habit to get into with your dog before you open the door to go outside or before you cross a busy street. An overly excited dog may want to bolt ahead, but a calm one will wait until he's been told it's safe to move forward.

INSTRUCTIONS

1. Start with your dog on a leash. Walk to the door and open it just an inch (2.5 cm). Say "Wait." (It doesn't matter whether your dog sits or stands.)
2. As soon as your dog pauses and looks away from the door, say "Good" and reward him with a treat.
3. Repeat five times.
4. As your dog begins to master this skill, increase how much you open the door and how long you make your dog wait.

OPTIONAL: **CLICKER TRAINING!**

Click when your dog looks away from the door and stays in place. Anytime you'd say "Good," give a click.

DR. GARY'S **TRAINING TIPS**

Once your pup has perfected this skill, release him from the waiting position by saying "OK." Then begin walking him through the door.

Go for a WALK

 Dogs love exploring the outdoors and, although it depends on your dog's breed and age, most need 30 minutes of exercise twice a day. The average kid needs at least 60 minutes of physical activity every day. These are two great reasons to get your dog's walking routine perfected.

INSTRUCTIONS

1 Put your dog on a leash. Tie or clip the leash to a stationary object so that he stays in place but can still see what you are doing.

2 Walk 25 steps away and place a treat or a toy on the ground.

3 Walk back to your dog, grab his leash, and begin walking slowly to the treat. If your dog runs too fast and pulls on the leash, start over. If he walks slowly to the treat, give it to him.

4 Repeat five times.

DON'T FORGET

to pick up your dog's poop when you're out for a walk! Never leave the house without dog waste bags. Stick your hand in the bag like a glove and pick up the poop with your covered hand. Then use your uncovered hand to pull the bag down and around the poop. Tie it in a knot and dispose of it in a trash can. Biodegradable pet waste bags can be found in pet stores or online and are better for the environment than plastic ones.

DR. GARY'S TRAINING TIPS

I like body harnesses instead of collars because they wrap around the middle section, which makes it easier to control a pet. Harnesses spread out the pressure of the leash, which makes it a little bit harder for larger dogs to pull and a little more comfortable for smaller dogs. They're especially good for puppies that can easily get tangled up in leashes!

HEEL

To "heel" means that your dog walks closely by your side. She should turn when you do, walk the same pace as you, and never run ahead of you. This is helpful for walks, especially when the two of you have to move through a crowded area with a lot of distractions. This training technique is best used for medium or large dogs.

INSTRUCTIONS

1 Put your dog on a short leash so she has to walk very close to you. Choose if you'd like her to stand on your right or left side.

2 Place five small treats in the hand that is nearest her. Ideally, your hand would be at the same level as your dog's nose.

3 Walk three steps.

4 On the fourth step (as long as she has walked with you), give her a treat.

5 Repeat five times.

6 When your dog begins to master this skill, add the cue "Heel" as she continues to walk by your side. Once she's mastered the skill, she should only need to be reminded of the cue when you need to get her attention back. For example, you may want to say "Heel" if, during a walk, she heads toward another dog across the street instead of staying by your side.

DR. GARY'S **TRAINING TIPS**

For this skill, you will want to walk at a quick, steady pace. Walking slowly will actually make this command harder to teach. And once you've chosen to walk your dog on your right or left side, stick to it.

Time for a CHECK-IN!

Dog training is hard work! Hopefully, by now you've spent a lot of quality time with your pup. Training is a great way to build up your friendship. Give yourself a pat on the back for being such a caring and thoughtful owner and for getting this far.

The two of you should be having a lot of fun practicing the basic commands. If it's stressful for either of you or moving a little slower than you thought, consider these questions:

- Have you been practicing 15 minutes total each and every day? (Three five-minute sessions a day are OK.)
- Are you using the same cues every time you practice?
- Are you quickly rewarding the correct behavior at the moment it happens instead of after?
- Are you practicing each skill at least five times in a row?
- Are you focusing on mastering one skill before moving on to the next?
- Are you practicing in a distraction-free environment?

DR. GARY'S TRAINING TIPS

Some dogs will only ever learn a few basic commands—and that's OK! It's a huge accomplishment to teach your dog these skills, and he'll be much better behaved because of it. Great job!

CANINE
Crime Fighters

Police officers often work in pairs for safety purposes—and sometimes that partner is a furry one. K-9 is short for "canine," which is another word for "dog." In K-9 units, police officers are matched with specially trained dogs that assist with crime-fighting duties like locating suspects or finding a missing person.

Dogs can be trained to find a very specific scent like that of a person's clothing or illegal items like drugs or explosives. When they do find something, the dogs sit or lie down near the object. A police dog's amazing nose can help an officer do his or her job faster. When it comes to fighting crime, acting fast is important.

Police dogs are really no different than any other officer. They report to work every day, and sometimes find themselves in dangerous situations. They are a huge help in keeping our communities safe.

Not just any dog—or any human—can join a K-9 unit. Police dogs and officers attend intense training programs and complete further schooling for specialized skills like tracking. Once they've passed a test and been certified, the pups and their human partners, also called handlers, continue to train every day. They often compete in local and national competitions to keep their skills sharp.

Some patrol pups return to a kennel at night where they can rest up for work the next day. Others go home with their handler each night. Just like their human counterparts, police dogs eventually retire, sometimes after as many as 10 years of service. And they may find themselves retiring at their partner's home. After years of working together, they've become family!

When a **police officer** works with **a dog,** it says **"K-9"** on the side of the patrol car.

NEVER PET a working police dog. He or she is on duty and shouldn't be distracted.

ADVANCED TRAINING

Has your dog mastered the basic skills? Excellent job! Now it's time to take your training up a notch. These commands build on the ones taught in the previous chapter. But they add an additional level of difficulty for your pup and for you.

While these skills might be a little bit more challenging, they are just for fun. You might call them "party tricks" because they'll be especially entertaining for your friends and family to watch at a party. But they are great entertainment anywhere.

Most dogs love to perform. They enjoy showing off the skills they've learned. It's interesting and exciting for them, which means it's good for their brains, and it's fun for the owners. Plus, both of you get great exercise.

The skills in this chapter can be learned in almost any order as long as your dog has already mastered the basic training on pages 40 to 63. We'll let you know if one advanced trick is required before learning another.

YOU NEED

- ▶ A quiet space free from distractions so you and your dog can focus
- ▶ An attentive dog (observe the signs of a happy dog on page 24)
- ▶ 15 minutes a day (can be spaced out in three five-minute sessions)
- ▶ Small and healthy treats for a reward
- ▶ Optional: a clicker

SHAKE

Well, isn't your dog polite! That's what people will think when they see him shaking your hand. For this trick, you'll have to decide whether you want your pup to shake with the left or right paw. Remember to use the same paw and hand every time you perform this trick.

INSTRUCTIONS

1. Command your dog into a "Sit" position (page 44).
2. Using your pointer finger, lightly tap the top of your dog's paw until he lifts it up.
3. When he begins to lift the paw, gently grab it with your hand and give it a small shake as you say "Shake."
4. Reward your dog with a treat.
5. Repeat five times.

Soon your dog will begin lifting his paw when you offer your hand or upon hearing the cue "Shake." You can also try this trick using the word "paw" instead of "shake."

In the United States, **44 percent** of households own a **dog.** That's almost **half** of all **homes.**

HIGH-FIVE

After learning how to shake, a high five isn't too far off. (Well, technically it's a high four!) A simple twist of the wrist turns one trick into another that is just as cute. Remember to use the same paw and hand every time you perform this trick.

INSTRUCTIONS

❶ Cue your dog to "Shake" (page 66) by simply offering your hand. Her paw should meet your hand.

❷ Try again, this time raising your hand a little higher and try again. Reward her when her paw meets yours.

❸ Repeat five times.

❹ Now flip your hand into a high-five position with your palm facing outward.

❺ When her paw meets your hand say "High-five," and give a treat.

❻ Complete steps 4 and 5 at least five times.

CAT

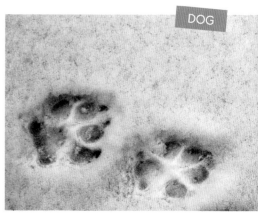

DOG

You can tell the **difference** between a **dog print** and a **cat print** by looking for **claw marks.** Cat tracks won't have claw marks because cats **retract** their claws when they walk.

SIT Pretty

"Sit pretty" means that a dog will sit on his rear end and raise his front paws like he's begging. Before you teach this skill, check with your veterinarian to make sure your dog doesn't have any back problems. This trick is not recommended for long-backed dogs like dachshunds and basset hounds. Even if your dog is healthy, don't practice too much because your pup will be working his muscles in a new way. It's good for him, but you don't want to over-work him.

INSTRUCTIONS

1. Cue your dog to "Sit" (page 44). Reward him with a treat.
2. Hold a treat a few inches over his head, then move it slightly back-ward so he must crane his neck. Eventually, his front paws will come off the ground.
3. As soon as his front paws leave the ground, say "Good" and give a reward. If he stands or jumps up, don't give him a treat and start over.

4. Repeat five times.
5. When your dog begins to master this skill, add the cue "Sit pretty" as you perform the trick together. Start with the cue just before he does it and give him a treat when he succeeds. You may need to revisit these steps a few times before he really masters this one. But once he has it down, he should be able to perform it with the verbal cue only.

DR. GARY'S **TRAINING TIPS**

If your dog has trouble balancing once he lifts his paws, let him rest his paws on your arm for a couple of seconds. Once your dog starts to master "Sit pretty," wait a second or two before rewarding him with a treat so that he holds the pose longer.

 OPTIONAL: **CLICKER TRAINING!**

Click the moment your dog raises his paws in the air. As he gets better at the trick, wait to click until he's held the position for a second or two.

SPIN

This command uses a treat to lure your dog around and around—almost like she's chasing her tail! A lure is an object that your dog wants to follow. By using a lure, the dog is encouraged to move a certain way. Not only will your friends and family love this party trick, but more important, your dog will love the attention she gets when she performs it.

INSTRUCTIONS

❶ Catch your dog's attention with a treat in your hand.

❷ Hold the treat just in front of her nose. Then slowly move your hand in a large circle above her head, so her nose follows your hand.

❸ If she follows your hand around in a complete circle, reward her with a treat.

❹ Repeat five times.

❺ When your dog begins to master this skill, add the cue "Spin" as you perform the trick together. Once she's mastered the skill, she should be able to perform it with the verbal cue only. The circular hand gesture will help too.

The smart and friendly **Labrador retriever** has been the **most popular** dog breed in America for **25 years.**

SPEAK

Your dog already barks all the time, right? But this time we're trying to teach her to bark on cue! The goal is to teach your dog how to bark only once, so don't reward her if she goes into a barking frenzy. First, you'll need a toy, a ball, or a treat that makes her super excited and likely to bark. If you have a particularly noisy dog, you may not want to teach this skill.

INSTRUCTIONS

1. Wave the toy, ball, or treat in front of your dog until she barks.
2. When she barks, immediately say "Good" and give her a treat.
3. Repeat five times.
4. When your dog begins to master this skill, add the cue "Speak" as you perform the trick together. Try saying it once you show her the ball, toy, or treat. When she's mastered the skill, she should be able to perform it with the verbal cue only.

One type of dog can't bark.
Basenjis are a type of hound found in Africa.
They're not totally silent, though.
They make a unique noise that is
similar to a yodel!

BASENJI

HUSH

Most dogs love to bark, but sometimes we'd like a little peace and quiet! The goal with this skill is to teach your dog that if he is quiet when you ask, it will earn him a treat. To teach this skill, you'll have to wait for your dog to start barking on his own.

INSTRUCTIONS

1. Listen to your dog bark and wait for him to stop.
2. When he stops, say "Good" and reward him with a treat.
3. Repeat the next time your dog barks. Unlike the other skills, this one could take months to teach.

4. When your dog begins to master this skill, add the cue "Hush" while your dog is barking. Wait for him to stop, then give a treat. In time, he should be able to perform it with the verbal cue only. Even better, you should eventually be able to give the cue when he's barking to focus his attention on you and the reward, not the mail carrier walking toward your house!

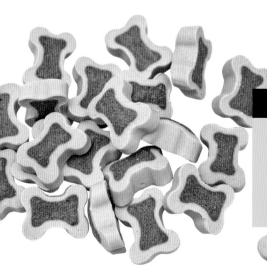

DR. GARY'S **TRAINING TIPS**

As you continue to practice, wait a second before giving him a treat. Slowly increase the amount of time he must be quiet until he earns a treat.

DR. GARY'S **TRAINING TIPS**

This skill also requires a release word like "OK" (page 46). Wait a few seconds before speaking the release word to encourage your dog to hold the position for a few seconds longer. Then quickly reward her with a treat.

PLAY
Dead

Once your dog knows how to lie down on command, you can teach her to "Play dead." It simply involves getting into the "Down" position (page 48) and then rolling slightly onto her side. Once she's mastered it, she'll be on her way to learning "Roll over" (page 80). Just like the "Spin" command (page 72), we'll use a treat as a lure to persuade your dog to move into the correct position.

INSTRUCTIONS

1. Cue your dog to "Sit" (page 44). Reward her with a treat.
2. Kneel directly in front of her, then hold a treat to the side of her head.
3. Now move the treat toward her shoulder so she lays down and rolls onto her side.
4. At that moment, give her the treat.
5. Repeat five times.
6. When your dog begins to master this skill, add the cue "Play dead" as you perform the trick together. Remember: Always give the cue before your dog starts the trick. Once she's mastered the skill, she should be able to perform it with the verbal cue only.

ROLL Over

This skill requires some coordination from your pup. First she'll need to sit on her hip, then tuck her shoulder, and of course, roll onto her back. A treat will help guide her through this process. It may be easier to succeed, and more comfortable for your canine pal, if you practice this one on a soft surface like carpet or grass.

INSTRUCTIONS

1. Cue your dog to get "Down" (page 48).
2. Place a treat near the side of her nose to encourage her to turn her head to the side. Keep moving the treat near her shoulder until her head lies flat on the ground.
3. Reward her with a treat.
4. Repeat five times.
5. Now repeat steps 1 and 2 but go further by moving the treat from her nose to her shoulder to her backbone, which will encourage her to roll onto her back.
6. Continue moving the treat until she's rolled onto the other side.
7. Reward her with a treat.
8. Complete steps 5 through 7 at least five times.
9. When your dog begins to master this skill, add the cue "Roll over" while she is lying down but just before she starts to roll onto her back. Once she's mastered the skill, she should be able to perform it with the verbal cue only (after you've completed step 1).

The saluki is one of the oldest dog breeds in the world. They are believed to have been very popular in ancient Egypt. Some were found mummified in tombs alongside their royal owners.

DANCE

 Can you imagine your dog twirling like a ballerina? With a little practice, he can. But it's not easy. Dancing is best for smaller dog breeds that are less than 30 pounds (14 kg). Like the "Sit pretty" trick (page 70), this one isn't for dogs with long backs. Standing on hind legs can be too stressful on a larger dog's body.

INSTRUCTIONS

1 Cue your dog to "Sit" (page 44). Reward him with a treat.

2 Hold a treat a few inches over his head, then move it slightly backward so he must crane his neck. Eventually, his front paws will come off the ground and he will begin standing on his hind legs.

3 As soon as he stands on his hind legs, say "Good" and give him a treat.

4 Repeat five times.

5 Now repeat steps 1 through 3, but move the treat in a circular motion above the dog's head once he is standing on his hind legs. This will encourage him to turn in a circular motion.

6 If he twirls correctly (in a complete circle), reward him with a treat.

7 Complete steps 5 and 6 at least five times.

8 When your dog begins to master this skill, add the cue "Dance" just before he starts turning around on his hind legs. Once he's mastered the skill, he should be able to perform it with the verbal cue only.

DR. GARY'S **TRAINING TIPS**

Dogs can get dizzy just like humans. So don't overpractice this trick and make sure to give your dog a break between sessions.

HUG

You know your pup loves you. But wouldn't it be nice if she could show it by giving you a hug? For this trick, the goal is to teach your pup to place her head against your shoulder for a few seconds. This command works best with medium to large dogs because small dogs are too tiny to reach your neck.

INSTRUCTIONS

1. Start by sitting on your bottom or knees so that you are eye level with your dog.

2. Place a treat in your hand, then place your hand behind your neck. Your pup will start to follow the treat, and her neck will rest alongside your neck.

3. Let her nibble at the treat, then let her have it (while still keeping your hand behind your neck).

4. Repeat five times.

5. When your dog begins to master this skill, add the cue "Hug" just before she leans in to get the treat. The goal is to start the trick with the cue before your dog starts to perform it. Once she's mastered the skill, she should be able to perform it with the verbal cue only.

A golden retriever named **Louboutina** became famous for offering hugs to anyone who'd walk by her busy city street corner. Now she's known as the **"Hugging Dog."**

DROP IT!

When your dog hears the cue "Drop it," she'll drop whatever is in her mouth. That might be a toy during a game of tug or something that's in her mouth but shouldn't be. To teach this trick, you'll need a toy and a handful of treats.

INSTRUCTIONS

- Give your dog a toy. Once it is in her mouth, hold a treat up to her nose.
- When your dog drops the toy, give her the treat and say "Good." (Don't remove the toy from her mouth. Wait for her to drop it. You want her to trade her toy for a treat willingly.)
- Repeat five times.
- Repeat five more times, but now say "Drop it" as you hold the treat near her nose. Gradually move the treat farther away from her nose. Reward her when she drops the toy.

Play TUG

Playing tug is fun! Not only is it a great game to play with your pet, but it can also lead to even cooler tricks. (Turn to page 112 to see how "Tug" can help your dog learn to open doors.) For this trick, you'll need a tug toy. To find out how to make your own tug toy, see page 148.

INSTRUCTIONS

1. Cue your dog to "Sit" (page 44). Reward her with a treat.
2. Show her the tug toy. Wave it around, then drag it across the ground to get her attention.
3. Once she's got her mouth on the toy, start gently pulling the other end of the tug toy and say "Good." Move the toy slowly from side to side and continue to say "Good."
4. Continue holding the toy with your hand. Say "Drop it" (see opposite page) to end the game. Bring a treat to her nose so she'll drop the toy and eat the reward. When she drops the toy say "Good."
5. Repeat five times.
6. When your dog begins to master this skill, add the cue "Tug" to start the game.

DR. GARY'S **TRAINING TIPS**

Every game has rules, and tug is no exception. Your dog must sit and wait for you to initiate the game with the word "tug." If she bites at the toy before then, walk away. She may growl a bit during playtime, which is completely normal, but if she begins to act aggressive, end the game. If she nips at you, immediately drop the toy and walk away.

CATCH

Playing catch is a little different for dogs. They catch with their mouths instead of their hands! For this trick, you'll start with small treats and then work your way up to a small, soft toy like a tennis ball. Be sure to use a toy that is safe for your dog and that does not break easily. Little dogs may only be able to master the treat-catching portion of this trick because most toys are just too big for them.

INSTRUCTIONS

1. Cue your dog to "Sit" (page 44) about two feet (60 cm) in front of you.
2. Hold a treat in your hand, and make sure your dog sees it. Toss the treat in the air toward your pup.
3. If she catches it in her mouth, great. If she doesn't, try to scoop it up before she gets it. Then she'll be motivated to catch it before it hits the ground.
4. Repeat five times.
5. When your dog begins to master this skill, add the cue "Catch" after she sits and as you perform the trick together. Once your dog has mastered catching treats in the air every time, move on to a small, soft toy like a tennis ball.

DR. GARY'S **TRAINING TIPS**

Dogs love playing catch and chewing toys, but these activities can be dangerous. Dogs can choke just like humans. Be careful when you're giving your dog treats or toys—both can be choking hazards. Make sure any ball you toss is too big to be accidentally swallowed. Always supervise your dog to make sure she does not eat the toy.

PEEKABOO

This game isn't just for babies. Dogs like it too. For this cute trick, your dog stands behind you, then walks through your legs when you call "Peekaboo!"

INSTRUCTIONS

1. Stand facing forward with your legs shoulder width apart. Your dog should stand or sit just behind you.
2. Bend at the waist and lower one arm between your legs with a treat in your hand. Call to your dog.
3. When she walks through your legs say "Peekaboo," and reward her with the treat. (Optional: Cue her to "Sit" [page 44] once she's walked through your legs and before you reward her with a treat.)
4. Repeat five times.
5. Once she's mastered the skill, she should be able to perform it with the verbal cue only, right after you've set up step 1.

Thirty of the past 45 U.S. **presidents** have been **dog owners.** That means dogs have lived in the **White House** in Washington, D.C., for **130 years!**

Time for a **CHECK-IN!**

Wow! Congrats on teaching your dog the basic commands, as well as tackling some advanced skills. You two don't need to have mastered all of the skills in this last section to move on. But before you try to take on expert-level commands, ask yourself these questions:

- Is my dog in good health and spirits? Did my veterinarian say it's OK to teach my dog some tricks beyond the basic commands?
- Does my dog seem interested and eager to learn new skills or tricks? Can I keep his attention for a five-minute training session?
- Has my dog mastered the basic commands? Is he able to repeat them on cue in various settings and with different people in my family?
- Am I still having fun spending time with my dog and teaching him new things? Do I look forward to our training sessions?

- Am I able to continue to dedicate at least 15 minutes a day to training my pup? Can I stick with it for an entire month?

If you answered "yes" to these questions, let's try some new tricks! If you answered "no" to more than one question, your time might be best spent continuing to practice and perfect the earlier skills your dog liked in this book.

DR. GARY'S **TRAINING TIPS**

Is your dog having a hard time picking up anything beyond the basics? Maybe he's reached his learning potential. That's OK! Every dog is different, and your dog may only have the ability to learn certain skills. You'll know your dog can't master something when he just doesn't get a particular trick after a month of consistent training. Instead of doing more, try perfecting the skills you've already taught him.

Snow-Loving
SLED DOGS

Can you imagine traveling through a snowy wilderness on a sled pulled by huskies? In Alaska, U.S.A., that used to be the most common way to get around!

During the 1900s, the Iditarod Trail served as the main road through Alaska. Teams of Alaskan huskies carried mail, goods, and people by sled through freezing temperatures and across roads that were too snowy and icy to reach by car.

One of the most famous sled dogs was named Balto. In 1925, he swiftly led a team of dogs through the final leg of a five-day relay from Anchorage to Nome. They were carrying precious cargo: medicine for children who were ill. Thanks to Balto's strength and speed, the children in Nome got their medicine on time and were saved. Today, you can find a statue celebrating Balto in New York City's Central Park.

Sled dogs are no longer commonly used for transportation, but a world-famous race celebrates the sport of sled dog racing. It was inspired by Balto's epic journey. Since 1973, teams have competed every March in the Iditarod Trail Sled Dog Race. Dog teams race about 1,000 miles (1,609 km) from Anchorage to Nome.

It takes more than a week for each team to complete the course, but that includes mandatory breaks throughout the race so the dogs can rest and get checkups from a veterinarian. Each team is made up of 12 to 16 dogs that line up in groups of two plus a musher. A musher is the person who stands at the rear of the sled and is considered the "driver." But the two front dogs get to set the pace and steer the pack!

Dog mushing is Alaska's official state sport.

LEARN THE LINGO!

Dog mushers train their dogs with these commands: "Gee" means "Turn right," "Haw" means "Turn left," and "Mush" means "Let's go!"

Due to the long trip and freezing temperatures, there is always concern for the dogs' health. With all that exercise, they need to be properly fed and hydrated. To protect their paws from ice and snow, they wear protective booties. Dog mushers also give their pups lots of encouragement during the long ride. Sometimes they even sing to them!

EXPERT TRICKS

ONCE YOU AND YOUR DOG have mastered the basic skills and have taken on some of the advanced ones too, you may be ready to move on to expert-level activities.

These commands are good for more than just party tricks. Although they are more challenging to teach, they can be really useful for any dog owner. Imagine if your dog could bring you his leash or put himself to bed. How cool would that be?

The next section is best for dogs who really love to learn and owners who really love to teach. If training came naturally for you and your dog, or if you two have really built up some trust and patience, give some of these a try. The teaching process for these is a little lengthier. It may involve stringing a few cues together or teaching your pup a more advanced concept. But if you and your pet are up for it, it's worth the effort in the end.

YOU NEED

▶ A quiet space free from distractions so you and your dog can focus

▶ An attentive dog (review the signs of a happy dog on page 24)

▶ About 15 minutes a day (can be spaced out in three five-minute sessions)

▶ Small and healthy treats for a reward

▶ Optional: a clicker

Some of the most **popular dog names** from recent years are Max, Charlie, Cooper, Bella, Lucy, and Daisy.

FETCH

 Did you know that dogs have a natural tendency to chase moving objects? That means if you throw a tennis ball, your dog might naturally run after it and grab it. Some dogs, without any training, will even automatically bring the ball back to you. These kinds of dogs are called retrievers.

If your dog doesn't naturally do this, you can still teach her how. Fetch is a two-part process: the retrieving part and the giving part. We'll cover the retrieving part here and the giving part on the following pages. To start, find a toy or ball your dog likes and that is easy for you to throw. (Turn to page 144 for instructions on how to make a DIY sock toy.) Remember, any balls thrown should be soft and never small enough to be swallowed.

INSTRUCTIONS

❶ Face your dog. Hold a ball directly in front of her. When she looks at the ball, offer a treat. Do this five times.

❷ Now hold the ball directly in front of her face. Wait for her to touch the ball with her nose. When she does, offer a treat. Do this five times.

❸ Hold the ball directly in front of her face again. Don't reward her for a look or a nose. Wait until she gets restless and grabs the ball with her mouth. Now offer a treat. Do this five times.

❹ Place the ball on the ground. When she touches the ball with her mouth say "Good" and then offer a reward. Do this five times.

❺ When your dog begins to master this trick, add the cue "Fetch" as you lay the ball on the ground.

❻ Now it's time to throw the ball. Start by saying "Fetch" when you have your dog's attention just before you throw the ball. Make sure you do this before she starts to run or she won't even hear the cue. Give her the treat when she brings the ball back to you. Once she's mastered the trick, she should be able to perform this with the verbal cue only.

OPTIONAL: **CLICKER TRAINING!**

If you're using a clicker, click at the moment your dog picks up the ball or toy and starts running back to you.

GIVE

The second part to playing fetch is "Give," when your dog returns the ball to you. Without "Give," you can't keep playing the game! For this command, you'll need a tennis ball or any soft toy that your dog loves to put in her mouth.

INSTRUCTIONS

1. Place your dog's favorite toy in front of you. Let her come and pick it up.
2. While holding a treat in one hand, say "Give" with your other palm open in front of your dog's mouth. Because she wants the treat, she'll drop the toy.
3. Say "Good" as she drops the toy and reward her with the treat.
4. Repeat five times.
5. Now throw her favorite toy in front of you and give the command "Fetch" (page 98). Let her run to it and pick it up. Say "Good" when she does. Practicing in an enclosed space like a hallway can be helpful during this step. Make sure the space is clear of furniture and other items so nothing falls if it is hit.
6. Now walk all the way to her. While holding a treat in one hand, say "Give" with your other palm open in front of your dog's mouth. Because she wants the treat, she'll drop the toy.
7. Complete steps 5 and 6 at least five times.

DR. GARY'S **TRAINING TIPS**

When you play fetch with your dog, you're using the Premack's principle, which means that highly desirable behaviors (like playing outside on a sunny day) will boost behaviors that are less desirable (like putting on sunscreen). Your dog loves chasing a ball much more than she loves giving you the ball. But to chase the ball, she'll also have to give it to you. That's how fetch works!

RING the Bell

 Wouldn't it be nice if you knew exactly when your dog needed to go to the bathroom? With this trick, you can! After some practice, your dog will let you know when she wants to head outdoors. First, you'll need a bell and a piece of string.

INSTRUCTIONS

1 Hold the bell close to your dog's nose. Shake it to get her interest. When she touches the bell with her nose and it rings, say "Bell" and offer a treat. Repeat five times.

2 Once she's mastered touching the bell, move it farther away from her nose so she has to walk a few steps to touch and ring the bell. Then give her the treat. Repeat at least five times.

3 Now tie a string to the bell and hang it from the doorknob of the door she uses to go outside. You may need to hold the string yourself near the door until she is used to going to the door to touch the bell.

4 Say "Bell" and reward her when she touches it with her nose. Complete steps 3 and 4 at least five times.

DR. GARY'S **TRAINING TIPS**

If you want your dog to ring the bell only when she needs to go to the bathroom—and not when she wants to play—you need to be strict. When she rings the bell, put her on a leash, take her outside to go to the bathroom, and then give her a treat. If she doesn't go to the bathroom within the first few minutes, come right back inside.

KEEP **PRACTICING!**

Now that she knows how to ring the bell, be sure to stop and request that she ring the bell before each trip outside to go to the bathroom. Soon she'll know that when she rings the bell, you will open the door.

BRING It

Once your dog understands the concept of "Fetch" (page 98), you can ask her to retrieve other things. You can teach your dog to bring you almost anything. For this trick, we'll have her retrieve her leash.

Before you begin, commit to keeping her leash in a location within her reach. Consider looping the leash and clipping it around itself so it's easy for her to grab.

INSTRUCTIONS

1 Begin training in the spot where her leash is kept. Hold the leash in a nice bundle in front of your dog. Shake it to get her interested. If she touches it with her nose, say "Good" and give her a treat. Repeat five times.

2 Now wait for your dog to touch the leash with her mouth. When she does, say "Leash" and give her a treat. Repeat five times.

3 Now set the leash where you intend to keep it. Say "Leash." When she touches the leash with her mouth, give her a treat. Do this at least five times.

4 Keep practicing until your dog picks up the leash with her mouth and holds it there. Reward her when she fully picks up the leash.

5 When your dog begins to master this trick, add the cue "Bring it" to teach your dog to bring her leash to you. Once she's mastered this trick, she should be able to perform with the verbal cue only. During practice, move yourself farther and farther away from the leash location.

6 Hold out your hand and cue "Give" (page 100) to accept the leash. Then quickly reward her with a treat. And don't forget to follow it up with the biggest reward of all: a walk with you!

DR. GARY'S **TRAINING TIPS**

"**B**ring it" is different than "Fetch" (page 98) because you're teaching your dog to get something that's stationary, or not moving. One part of this trick is teaching your dog that it's OK to put the item in her mouth. Another part is making an object interesting to her so your dog wants to grab it. If your dog seems uninterested in the object, try shaking it in front of your pup's face then set it down right in front of her. Give the command "Bring it" immediately after the item is set down and stops moving.

OPTIONAL: **CLICKER TRAINING!**

If you are using a clicker, click or use a marker word exactly when your dog reaches the designated spot. Then give a treat.

PLACE

Teaching a dog "Place" is helpful for when you're leaving the house or when visitors are arriving. It keeps your dog from running out the door or jumping on guests. Choose a spot near, but not too near, the door you use the most.

As you get ready to leave the house or just before friends and family walk through the door, you can instruct your pup to his "Place" where he can "Sit" (page 44) and then "Stay" (page 46) peacefully.

INSTRUCTIONS

1. Stand in the spot that will become your dog's "place." Call to your dog. When he arrives to the specific spot, say "Place" and give him a treat. Do this five times.
2. Now pat the specific spot and say "Place." When your dog comes to it, give him a treat. Do this five times.
3. Step away from the designated spot and stand near the door. Say "Place."
4. Once your pup walks to the designated spot, walk to him and reward him with a treat. To release your dog from this position, say "OK" (page 46).
5. Complete steps 3 and 4 at least five times.

Corgis roamed the halls of Buckingham Palace in London, England, for more than 80 years!

Go to **BED**

This trick comes in handy at the end of the day, of course, but it's also useful for when your dog is misbehaving—or just before he misbehaves. When you say "Bed," your dog will know to find his bed, lie down, and stay there until he's been released. For this trick, you'll need a designated spot for your dog to sleep, like a dog bed or a crate. (You could also use the word "crate" as a cue instead of "bed.")

INSTRUCTIONS

1. Using a treat as a lure, encourage your dog to walk toward his bed and step on top of it.
2. Cue him to go "Down" (page 48), then drop a treat onto the bed just between his paws. Release him with "OK" (page 46).
3. Repeat five times.
4. Now walk toward the bed and see if your dog will follow you. Hopefully, he will get on the bed and lie down. If he does, give him a treat while he's still lying on the bed. If he doesn't, practice steps 1 and 2 a few more times.
5. When your dog begins to master this trick, add the cue "Bed" as you perform the trick together. Say this just before he climbs onto the bed. Once he's mastered the trick, he should be able to perform it with the verbal cue only and walk over to the bed on his own.

DR. GARY'S **TRAINING TIPS**

Before you begin teaching this trick, you may want to leave a few treats on the bed occasionally. That way your dog will find them on his own and learn that the bed is a good place to be.

Once your dog begins to walk to his bed without being lured there with a treat, take a few steps away from the bed. Reward him if he stays by throwing another treat onto the bed. Eventually, the goal is to send him to bed even if you are standing in another room in the house.

DR. GARY'S **TRAINING TIPS**

Mastering this one trick could take your dog more than a week. You may want to practice in five-minute training sessions three times a day. Don't rush this trick, and don't raise the hoop too high. Put your dog's safety first!

Jump Through a **HOOP**

This one's a showstopper! For this trick, you'll need a hula hoop. Before you begin, ask your veterinarian if your dog is strong enough to jump. Puppies or older dogs may have bones that are too weak. But the size of your dog is not a problem. While it may be easier for bigger dogs, small dogs can do this trick too because we'll hold the hoop very low to the ground.

INSTRUCTIONS

1. Crouch down and hold the hula hoop upright with one side touching a wall. The bottom of the hula hoop should touch the floor. With this placement, your dog won't have much of a choice but to walk through it.

2. With a treat in your other hand, lure your dog toward the hoop. Then toss the treat through the hoop. Make sure it lands a couple feet past the hoop so your dog has to walk all the way through the hoop to get the treat.

3. As your dog follows the treat and steps through the hoop say "Good." Repeat at least five times.

4. Now lift the hoop an inch (2.5 cm) off the floor. Complete steps 2 and 3 at least five times.

5. When your dog begins to master this trick add the cue "Jump" as soon as you have set up the hula hoop. Once he's mastered the trick, he should be able to perform it with the verbal cue only.

LEARN ABOUT agility courses and how you can incorporate tricks like this one into a fun obstacle course challenge for your pup by turning to page 152.

Open a **DOOR**

Can a dog really open a door?
Well, kind of. It's a complex trick
that even some professional trainers
have trouble mastering. But when they
do, the results are awesome!

For this trick, we'll tie a rope to a
door handle. When the dog pulls on
the rope—ta-da! The door will open.
This trick is best for doors, or crate
doors, that you only have to pull to
open. Check to be sure that there is
nothing on the other side of the door
that could fall on or injure your pup.

Before you begin, teach the "Tug"
command on page 87.

INSTRUCTIONS

❶ Attach a rope to a door handle or
to the door of your dog's crate.

❷ Close the door. Lift or wave around
the end of the rope to catch your
dog's attention. When she touches
it with her mouth, say "Good" and
reward her with a treat.

❸ Complete step 2 at least five times.

❹ When your dog begins to master
this trick, add the cue "Pull" as
soon as she mouths the rope. Give
a treat every time she grabs the
rope with her mouth and pulls
it. Once she can both mouth and
pull the rope, she should be able to
perform it with the verbal cue only.

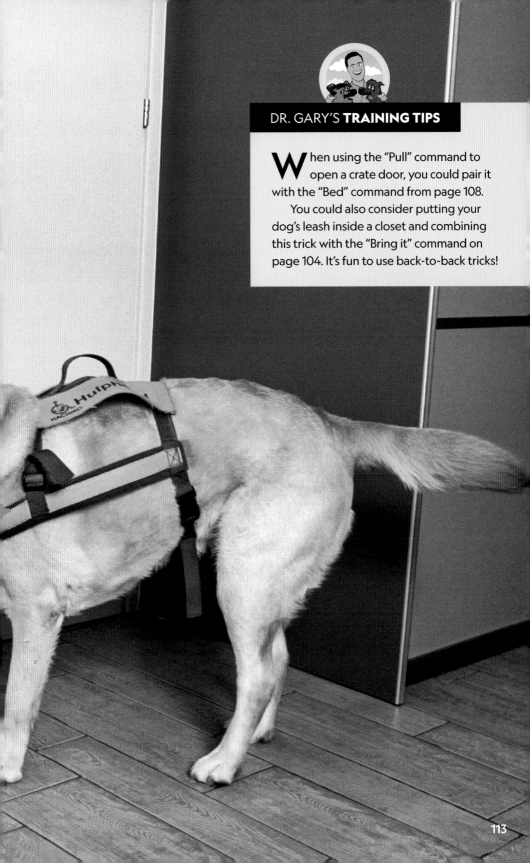

DR. GARY'S **TRAINING TIPS**

When using the "Pull" command to open a crate door, you could pair it with the "Bed" command from page 108. You could also consider putting your dog's leash inside a closet and combining this trick with the "Bring it" command on page 104. It's fun to use back-to-back tricks!

Surfing PETS

Every year, the city of Huntington Beach, California, U.S.A., hosts a famous surfing competition. Surfers from all over the world compete—and so do sur-*furs*. That's right. Dogs take on the waves too!

A local beach turns into the site of a thrilling competition when dozens of dogs hop on surfboards. Spectators—of the human and furry kind—cheer on the competitors, which include French bulldogs, poodles, border collies, Labrador retrievers, Chihuahuas, pit bulls, and more.

The competition is divided into rounds where dogs compete by size and in certain categories. In the tandem categories, you could find a human and a dog surfing together or two dogs surfing together on one board. Professional surfing judges grade the competitors on the length of the ride, the height of the wave, and the difficulty of the maneuvers.

Owners are always standing nearby in the water. After all, dogs can't paddle out into the ocean on their own, and their boards need a good push to catch a wave. Every dog is required to wear a life vest because safety comes first!

⚠️ SAFETY FIRST

BEFORE YOU GO into the water be sure you have an adult nearby to supervise. Remember, **not every dog** can swim. Talk to your vet before allowing your dog near an ocean, lake, or pool. If your dog is going in the water, never put him on a leash. It's very dangerous because the leash could get caught on something underwater. And remember, dogs that surf are trained by experts. Don't try this trick with your dog!

These pups are true **celebrities** in this **surf contest.** There's even a **red carpet** for them to walk the night before.

PROBLEM-SOLVING

I**T'S NOT UNCOMMON** for a dog to pick up some bad habits. Those habits might range from pulling on the leash during a walk to peeing in the house. Things don't always go our way when it comes to our pets' behavior. But there is something we can do about it.

The best way to change these behaviors is to teach your dog what he can do instead. For example, if you don't want your dog to jump on visitors, what is a good behavior that he could do when visitors arrive? Maybe he could learn to sit patiently by the door. Now you can move your focus to rewarding the good behavior (instead of punishing the bad), which is a better way to teach your dog good manners.

Another consideration is to remove the option for the bad behavior to happen in the first place. For the same dog that jumps on visitors, maybe it's better if he's brought into another room when guests walk through the front door. Now he can't jump on anyone. A little help like this can go a long way in raising a well-trained pup.

No Such Thing as a "BAD DOG"

 Dogs aren't born with the ability to behave as you'd like them to: They have to be taught. That's where training comes in. If a dog chews your shoes or refuses to come when called, remember these are just his natural tendencies. He can't help it—until you teach him differently.

A lot of factors determine how your dog behaves. Your dog is born with some of them, and others have to do with your dog's environment. Here are some factors that can affect your pet's temperament:

- **SOCIALIZATION:** When your dog was a puppy did he hang out with other pets, kids, and adults?
- **EXERCISE:** Does he get about 30 minutes of exercise twice a day?
- **NEGATIVE EXPERIENCES:** Did he have a traumatizing, or very upsetting, experience at the vet or with a past owner?
- **PRIOR LEARNING:** Have you or a previous owner (accidentally) taught your dog some bad habits?

DR. GARY'S **TRAINING TIPS**

Dogs have a lot of humanlike characteristics, such as the ability to make memories, learn skills, and sense emotions. But remember: Dogs aren't human. Even the smartest dog can't be expected to understand everything a human would. Avoid saying things like "He knows better!" and don't assume that your dog comprehends every word you say. He doesn't. All he knows for sure is that he wants to please you.

Should I **PUNISH** My Pup?

Never punish your dog. If you're considering punishing your pet, it's probably because you want her to stop a certain behavior. But studies have found that it's better to reward, or reinforce, good behavior instead of punishing the bad.

There's a reason why behavioral scientists recommend positive reinforcement, like giving a treat when your pup sits on command instead of scolding her when she doesn't sit. This is a more effective way to train your dog because it's less confusing. Also, she likely won't understand that the thing she just did was considered bad behavior.

But come on, we all know that sometimes your dog misbehaves. She won't listen to commands, and there is no good behavior to reward. Disciplining your dog can simply mean taking something away that brings her happiness—just like if you weren't allowed any screen time for a week because your room was messy. This is called negative punishment because it means that something is taken away to keep the behavior from happening again.

For example, when your dog barks too much, you could leave the room. She wanted your attention and now she can't get it. Her reward, which was your attention, was removed. If she wants it back, she will have to stop barking.

If you're in the middle of a training session and your dog is not cooperating, you can "cancel" the treat, which simply means to put the treat away and start over. You could also give your dog a short break or end the training session completely.

And if your dog rings the bell to go outside—but then doesn't really have to go to the bathroom—bring her inside immediately. Her reward, which was playing outside, can only happen after she goes to the bathroom.

If you keep these tips in mind, your dog can learn faster and be a happier, more well-behaved pup. And you'll be a happier owner! Turn the page to see some of these strategies in action.

PULLING
on a Leash

Boy, is going for a walk exciting! Your dog takes in so many sights and sounds and smells. Every squirrel, tree, or person is like a reward for his senses. Sometimes it feels like your dog is taking you for a walk.

In an ideal world, your dog would keep the leash loose as the two of you walk together. But we all know that dogs don't always heel. If the "Heel" command (page 58) isn't working on a walk, try stopping in your tracks each time your dog pulls on the leash. Don't start walking again until he moves closer to you and puts some slack back on the leash. He'll soon realize that to explore the world, he needs to remain close to you. Once he begins walking and stays close, reward him with a treat every few steps just like with the "Heel" command.

The hardest part about correcting this behavior is that it must be addressed each and every time it happens. So, every time the dog pulls on the leash, you must stop walking. It can be frustrating for both of you at first, but soon your dog should get the hang of it.

Remember to keep those treats on hand so you can quickly reward the good behavior.

DR. GARY'S **TRAINING TIPS**

When taking your dog for a walk, attach your leash to a harness instead of a collar. A harness puts less pressure on your dog's throat during the instances when he tugs on his leash, and it can help you better control a strong pup as he pulls away.

JUMPING
Up on Guests

 Your dog jumps on anyone who walks through the door, and she won't stop even though everyone tells her to get down. What gives? Your pup is probably looking for attention. Even though you are telling her to stop, she is getting your attention. She doesn't mind if it's the negative kind. To prevent your pup from continuing this behavior, start practicing the "Sit" command (page 44) with some distractions.

INSTRUCTIONS

1. Place your dog on a leash and cue her to "Sit." Reward her with a treat when she listens.
2. Now ask a friend or family member to walk slowly toward your pup.
3. If she stays sitting while the other person approaches, reward her with a treat! If not, try again.
4. Repeat at least five times.

DR. GARY'S **TRAINING TIPS**

Once your dog can stay sitting while someone approaches, practice having that person enter through the front door. Make sure your pooch remains seated next to you. If she stands up, ask your helper to leave and close the door. When your pup sits calmly as a person enters, reward her with a treat. Eventually, it won't matter who walks in the front door, your dog will stay seated!

PEEING in the House

When it comes to potty training pups, know that dogs have only one rule: "Don't pee where you sleep." To them, peeing inside or outside doesn't matter as long as it's not on their own bed.

Just like other bad behaviors, the best thing you can do is try to prevent it from happening in the first place. That can be done by watching your dog very closely. If your dog starts sniffing, squatting, or circling (which could be signs that he needs to go to the bathroom), bring him outside immediately. Reward him with a "good dog" acknowledgment when he relieves himself outside successfully. In this case, don't reward with a treat because otherwise your dog might go outside just to get a treat instead of to go to the bathroom. Or he might cut his pee short to get the treat faster.

If your dog continues to pee or poop in the house, there is good news and bad news. Pups like to go to the bathroom in the same place over and over again. So if they went on the rug once, they'll probably do it again. To prevent peeing in the house, be sure to clean up each mess very, very well. The idea is to remove the scent completely from your carpet or flooring.

If your dog can smell it—remember he has a very good sense of smell—he will pee there again.

First soak up the pee with paper towels. Then spray the area with a mix of one cup (250 mL) distilled white vinegar and one cup (250 mL) cold water. (Have an adult help you mix the solution and clean up the mess.) Let it sit a few minutes before you blot it with a towel.

When cleaning up poop from a carpet or rug, wear rubber gloves and use paper towels. Pick up the solid pieces and dispose of them in the toilet, or consider trying this trick: Pick up the poop and bring it outside to where you'd like your dog to go to the bathroom. He'll follow the scent the next time he heads outside. Don't forget to clean it up after he sees and smells it. Every time you take your dog outside, put him at this spot.

To handle the poop stain, pour a small amount of club soda on top, let it fizz, and then lightly blot it with a paper towel. Repeat one more time. Then lightly blot the stain with a paper towel and a small amount of dishwashing soap. Finish with one more club soda rinse and blot. A store-bought pet stain spray will also work to clean up any messes.

DR. GARY'S **TRAINING TIPS**

Keep a consistent schedule as to when you take your dog outside to go to the bathroom, such as first thing in the morning, after meals, and just before bed. The consistency will help your pup better control bathroom breaks. Dogs might need a special bathroom trip after a nap or play session too.

ALWAYS WASH your hands after cleaning up after your dog.

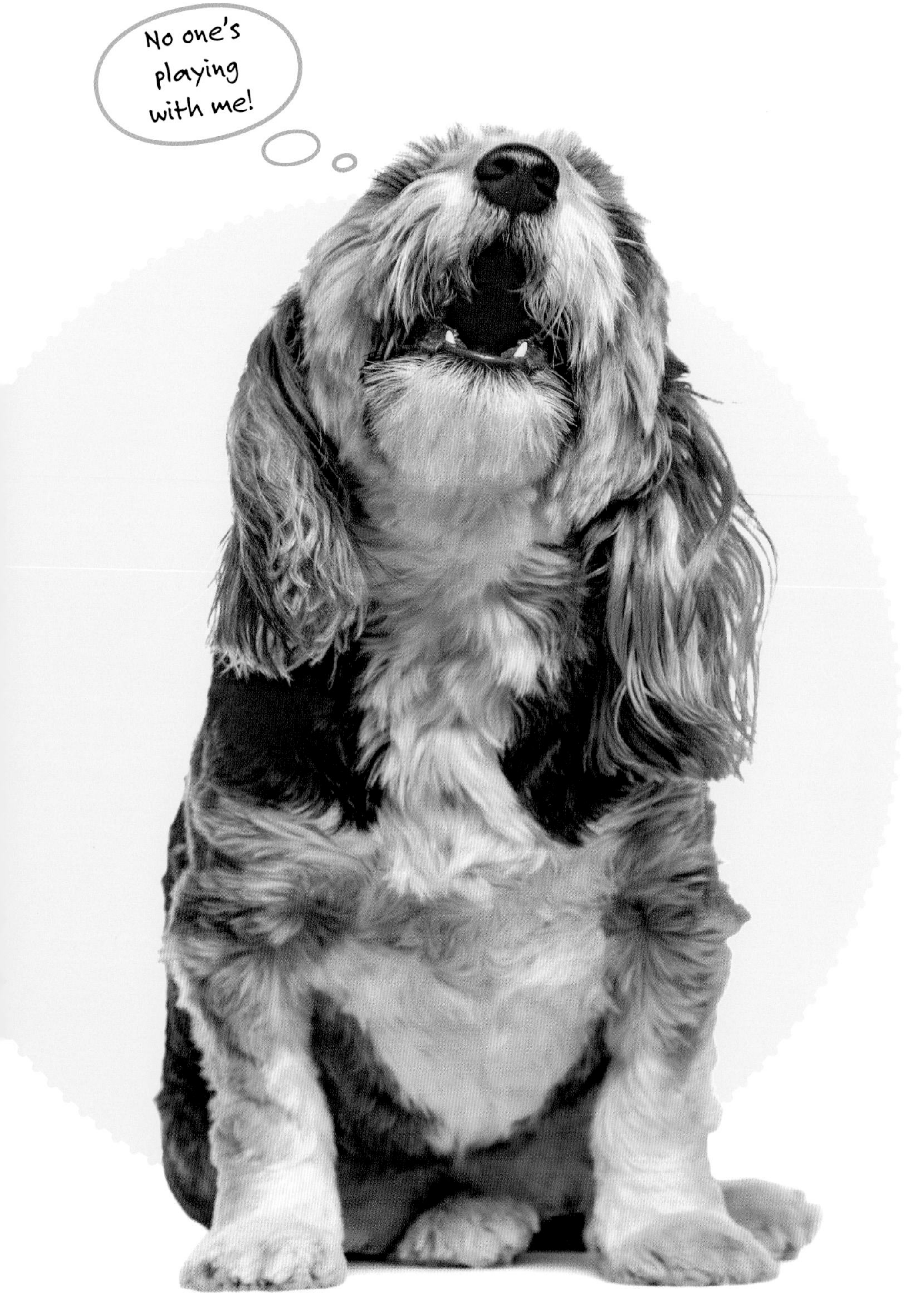
No one's playing with me!

BARKING

Barking is a completely natural behavior. But sometimes dogs bark at times that we don't like. And they bark a lot. Maybe even too much. With a little help, your dog can learn some self-control.

The first step is finding out what's causing your dog to bark—the "trigger." Our goal will be to remove the trigger, so your dog will bark less. Think about where your dog is barking, when he is barking, and who or what he might be barking at. He could be barking at animals or people.

If your dog is barking at something outside, you could close the curtains to prevent him from seeing what is happening out there. That may make him stop. If your dog barks when he is home alone, he might be bored. Give him a hidden treat dispenser toy to keep him busy. Also, try to add more cuddle time and exercise when the two of you are together.

If you think your dog is barking just to get attention, try not to give him any. Remember that even yelling or shushing your dog is considered attention to him. He doesn't realize that it's bad attention. To him, your attention is a reward! Instead, leave the room or look away. Reward him with a treat when he stops barking.

IS YOUR DOG barking at a sound outside—like a car alarm or a thunderstorm—that you can't stop? This is a good time to start up a training session to direct your dog's attention away from the noise. You could also go for a walk, turn on the TV, or turn up some tunes.

The pitch, length, and frequency of **barking patterns** are fairly standard across all **dog breeds,** unlike humans who speak many **different** languages.

JUMPING
Up on Counters

Mmmm ... smells good! That's probably what your dog is thinking when he jumps up on a counter or a table. He wants that food! Even the dirty dishes can be licked. And he's seen where you hide treats. If only he could reach a little bit farther ...

You can see why the kitchen would be a dangerous place for a dog to be. Kitchens offer a lot of opportunities for dogs to get into trouble. One of the easiest ways to correct this behavior is to set up a baby gate that blocks off access to the kitchen. This way your dog can't get into trouble in the first place.

If it isn't possible to set up a baby gate, go out of your way to keep food off the counters—that includes dirty plates, bags of snacks, and anything else that might catch your dog's eye (or nose!). When food is being cooked or eaten, offer a favorite toy in another room so your dog is distracted.

If you would rather keep your dog in the same room as your family while you eat dinner, try putting your dog on his leash and attaching it to a heavy piece of furniture. Place a comfy dog bed and a toy nearby. Or, if you'd prefer not to use a leash, practice the "Place" command (page 106) during dinnertime.

Your dog has a natural desire to eat any food in sight, including some foods that can make him sick. But if you keep the food away from the dog and the dog away from the food, you can help curb this habit.

"Throw 'em a bone!" is a common phrase that means to give someone something of little value in order to stop his or her complaining.

Won't Come When **CALLED**

"Come" (page 42) is a simple command, but it's an easy one to mess up during the training process. You may have taught your dog a few bad habits without even realizing it. Really put yourself in your dog's shoes, er, paws, and think about it from his perspective.

If your dog is outside, he's surrounded by all the distractions in the world. Why would he want to come back inside when there's a bird on the roof, a pile of crunchy leaves beside him, and what's that smell—is the neighbor cooking a chicken? To tempt him to come in, you'll have to give him a big reward—something much better than whatever is going on outside. Consider a fun toy or a handful of his favorite treats. Otherwise, coming inside will seem like a punishment.

If your dog is inside, the same rules apply. It may seem like there is no good reason that he shouldn't get up and come to you when called. But there are still a ton of distractions inside a home. Any TV, music, conversations between your family members, or tempting views outside the window can make it hard for him to focus on you.

Speaking of punishments, do not scold your dog once he finally does come. You should reward him for listening—even if on the 10th try. He won't want to come to you next time if he thinks he'll get in trouble.

Also, make sure you are being consistent when calling your dog. The command is simply "Fido, come." Don't yell his name over and over again. And don't repeat variations of the cue "Come," such as "Come here" or "Get over here" or "Come on now." He doesn't know what those mean. Stick to your one command and be firm but happy when you speak it.

If he still doesn't come, walk closer to him, then start jogging backward so he is tempted to run toward you. Use the command "Fido, come." Then offer him a treat when he does. Remember to always offer a treat when he comes inside.

CHEWING
Your Belongings

Before new parents bring a baby home, they often "baby-proof" the house by covering up electrical outlets, locking cabinet doors, and removing breakable items from low shelves. If you have a dog that likes to chew on things, you should think of "dog-proofing" your home in a similar way.

As you've already read, one of the easiest ways to stop bad behaviors is by preventing them from happening in the first place. That means putting things that he chews out of reach or behind closed doors. Shoes always go in the closet with the door closed. Socks always go in the dirty clothes hamper. Toys always go back in the toy chest.

Chewing is the most natural behavior in the world for a dog. Try leaving a variety of new and exciting chew toys out for your dog, especially in the rooms where he's usually looking for something to chew. Teething pups have sore gums and often like to chew on things because it's soothing. An older dog that chews a lot could be bored. Toys can help keep him entertained, especially if you switch them up often. You could also try taking him out for an extra walk or play session.

If you can't dog-proof your whole home, dog-proof one room that he can play in without harm. Or help keep him out of certain rooms that aren't dog-proofed by closing the door or putting up a baby gate. Remember that your dog doesn't know better. Setting him up for success is the best way you can help change his behavior.

Puppies grow 28 tiny teeth as early as two weeks of age. Around three to four months of age, those teeth fall out to make room for 48 adult teeth.

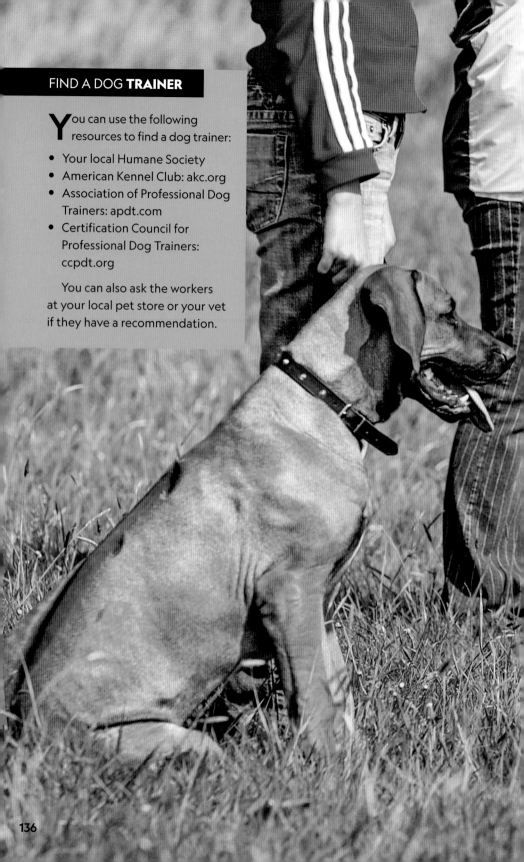

FIND A DOG **TRAINER**

You can use the following resources to find a dog trainer:

- Your local Humane Society
- American Kennel Club: akc.org
- Association of Professional Dog Trainers: apdt.com
- Certification Council for Professional Dog Trainers: ccpdt.org

You can also ask the workers at your local pet store or your vet if they have a recommendation.

Your Dog Needs MORE Help

Your pup might be stubborn and set in his ways. Or maybe he's scared and is having a tough time learning and trusting others. Perhaps he's mastered a few simple skills but you'd like him to learn more advanced tricks.

When this happens, a professional can help. Obedience classes, where dogs learn to follow commands, are offered at shelters, local pet stores, and obedience schools. They are usually once a week for about two months and are often taught by certified dog trainers. You'll likely be in a class with other owners and their pups where you will all learn together.

Even in a group class, the dog trainer should work closely with you and your pet. The goal is to teach you how to talk to your dog and to teach your dog how to listen. During the classes, you'll learn basic commands and skills like how to go on a walk together. You'll be expected to practice between classes. Yes, there's homework!

Obedience classes are great for puppies as young as two months old (once they've started on their vaccines) because they get a chance to learn good habits before bad ones start and they get to socialize, or play, with other dogs and people. It's important that this behavior work begins as early as possible. That's because after four months, a puppy will have learned most of his basic social skills. But the classes work for older dogs too. Trainers can help you and your pet work together to correct any problems or bad behaviors.

If your dog needs more one-on-one help or has more serious behavior problems, a private class may be best. The instructor can work directly with you and your dog. Your veterinarian can also answer any questions and can guide you to the best resources and help in your town.

Formal dog training classes don't have to be a onetime thing. You could take your dog to obedience classes or advanced skills and agility classes once your dog has mastered the basics. This is a great way to build the bond between you and your pup. The more you practice, the better your dog will behave!

SERVICE Animals

Service dogs protect and help their owners. These dogs are trained to perform tasks that assist an owner who has a physical or mental disability. Service dogs help their owners with things like sleeping, walking, eating, or dressing. These well-trained dogs are so important because their owners wouldn't be able to get through the day without them.

Because the owner needs assistance, service animals are allowed to go wherever their human goes—even places that usually won't allow dogs, like movie theaters, hospitals, and restaurants. People can even bring their dog to work or school every day.

These dogs are trained to help in any way the owner needs it. They have all sorts of daily responsibilities like pushing a wheelchair, opening a door, and reminding an owner to take medicine. They can also fetch important items like house keys or a telephone. There are many different kinds of service dogs, including the following:

- Guide dogs, or Seeing Eye™ dogs, help people who are blind or visually impaired get around safely, like when they cross the street, for example.
- Hearing or signal dogs assist people who are deaf by alerting them to sounds, like when someone knocks at the front door.
- A seizure response dog or psychiatric service dog can stand guard and protect his owner while she is feeling sick. The dog can also go get help.

CAN MY DOG **DO THAT?**

If your dog hasn't been trained to perform a necessary task for someone with a disability, then she won't qualify as a service animal. But it turns out that she can still be helpful to your health and well-being.

Research has found that spending time with a furry friend is calming. The act of petting an animal can be therapeutic. It can even boost your immune system and make you less likely to get sick. So, it turns out that your pet can provide comfort just by being her cute self!

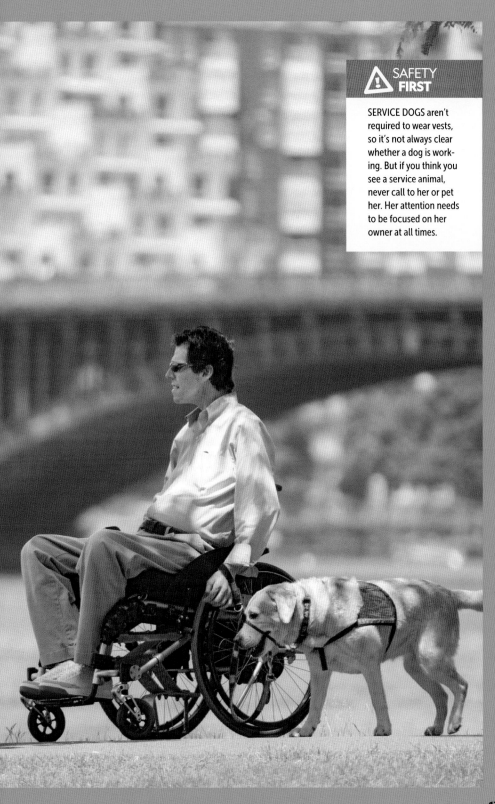

EXTRA CREDIT

YOUR DOG NEEDS to learn and needs to move. That's why playing is such an important part of raising a happy and healthy dog. During a good play session, your pup's mind and body get a workout.

Simply putting your dog in the same room as a toy and hoping she interacts with it is not enough. You have to find ways for your dog to use playtime to improve her physical and mental health.

This process is called enrichment. Enrichment stimulates an animal's senses, challenges her mind, and fulfills her need to be social. It also helps the two of you strengthen your bond. Enrichment can include daily walks, social interactions with other dogs and humans, food games, sounds, textures, and odors that stimulate your dog's senses.

Enrichment is also a great way to practice commands in a fun way. Some pets won't even need to be rewarded with treats during a play session—the activity itself is the reward. And, of course, the attention from you!

Be sure to observe what kinds of activities your dog responds to. Maybe she likes action-packed games that involve running around the backyard. Or perhaps she prefers quieter games that are more mentally challenging, like a treat dispenser toy. Then again, she might like both! Find the mix that makes your dog most happy.

Dog TOY GUIDE

Just like a kid, your dog likes a variety of toys. Each kind of toy helps your dog play and learn in a different way. Think about rotating your dog's toys every week so he always has something new to play with. While many of these toys give your pup great exercise, none of these should be a replacement for your daily walks together.

Plush Toys

Sometimes dogs need cuddling and soothing time. These soft toys can provide comfort, just like stuffed animals or a favorite pillow may provide comfort to you. Even a blanket or T-shirt that smells like you can be especially calming to your dog.

Chew Toys

Dogs love to chew. Chewing can relieve stress and help reduce the pain for teething puppies. But dogs shouldn't chew on just anything. Bones used to be popular chew toys, but your pup could easily crack a tooth or swallow a sharp piece. Hard rubber toys that are made for dogs are safer. Always supervise your dog when he uses a chew toy.

⚠️ SAFETY FIRST

NEVER LEAVE your dog unattended with a toy. Dogs have strong jaws and teeth so there is always a chance they can bite or rip through a toy and accidentally swallow it. If your dog eats something he shouldn't have, take him to the nearest veterinarian or an emergency animal clinic immediately.

Fetch Toys

These kinds of items—which include balls, flying discs, and soft toys—are great for throwing and retrieving. They should be lightweight, so they don't harm your dog if he's accidentally hit with one that's thrown. Make sure the toys are easy for your dog to pick up with his mouth so he can bring them back to you.

Puzzle Toys

Some toys have treats hidden within them. A dog must chew or paw the treat dispensers over and over again until the treat is released. These kinds of toys can keep dogs busy for longer periods of time—and keep them out of trouble. They're great for dogs that get bored easily and can distract them from barking or chewing.

DR. GARY'S **TRAINING TIPS**

Make sure the toy is the appropriate size for your dog—small enough that he can pick it up, but not so small that he might swallow or choke on it.

143

DIY Sock Toys

 It's no secret that dogs love socks. Owners of puppies will tell you—don't leave one on the ground! Before you know it, your pup's tiny teeth are chomping away. But these simple do-it-yourself (DIY) tips give your dog his very own special sock chew toy. Be sure to ask permission from your family before you turn an old sock into a toy.

Sock Sling

HOW TO MAKE: Slip a tennis ball into the foot of an old, long sock. Tie a knot just above the tennis ball so it can't slip out.

HOW TO USE: Holding the long end, fling the ball into the air and cue your dog to "Fetch" (page 98). Your dog may have an easier time picking up the long end of the sock in his mouth rather than the ball itself.

Knotted Rope

HOW TO MAKE: Tie a tight knot near the foot of an old, long sock. An inch or two above that knot, tie another tight knot. Repeat until you reach the end of the sock.

HOW TO USE: Dogs like to chew on knotted ropes. To them, it's a treat! If your dog really loves it, you can even reward good behavior with some quality time with a chew toy. Or turn to page 87 where you can find the command for "Tug" and learn how to play a tugging game with your pup.

Your dog might not be able to tell the difference between these sock toys and your real socks, so make sure you keep your own socks off your bedroom floor. Otherwise your pet might steal a pair while you're trying to get ready for school!

DR. GARY'S **TRAINING TIPS**

Remember how dogs see color differently from humans? Use a sock that's blue or yellow. Your dog will be able to see it much better than a red sock, especially when it's lying in the grass.

CATCH a Flying Disc

If your dog loves retrieving, you may be able to kick things up a notch by teaching her how to catch a flying disc made of dog-safe materials. This game is best for medium-size or large dogs that are at least one year old. Small pups are just too little to pick up a flying disc.

Before you begin playing with your dog, practice throwing the flying disc. You have to be able to throw it well, so he can catch it! When tackling this trick, always play outside. Flying discs aren't meant to be thrown inside the house. Find an open space away from cars and crowds of people.

For this trick, you will have to make sure your dog has mastered the "Fetch" (page 98) and "Give" (page 100) commands.

INSTRUCTIONS

1 Begin outside. Place the flying disc on the ground. When your dog mouths it, say "Good" and offer a treat. Repeat this five times.

2 Now try rolling the disc along the ground away from you. When your dog mouths it, say "Good" and offer a treat. Repeat this five times. Then practice adding the cue word "Fetch."

3 Now try throwing the disc a few feet in front of you. When your dog mouths it, walk to him, say "Good," and offer a treat. Repeat this five times. Use the cue word "Give" (page 100) to encourage your dog to give the disc back to you.

4 Keep practicing. Eventually, only reward your pup when he catches the flying disc in midair.

Disc dog is a sport that has been played since the 1970s. During official competitions, you can see dogs **jump off** of their owners' bodies and **lunge high into the air** to catch a flying disc.

DIY Rope Tug Toy

With strips of fleece, you can easily braid your own rope tug toy. Turn to page 87 where you can find the command for "Tug," and learn how to play a game with your pup. This tug toy can also be attached to a door handle or cabinet knob. It's perfect for the "Open a Door" training on page 112.

YOU NEED:

- ½ yard (0.5 m) of bulk fleece* in two different colors
- Scissors
- A friend

INSTRUCTIONS

❶ With an adult, cut the fabric into six strips, each measuring one inch (2.5 cm) wide and 18 inches (46 cm) long.

❷ Stack the strips of fabric on top of each other and tie the end in a knot.

❸ Place the knotted fabric on a flat surface. Ask a friend to hold the knotted end.

❹ Separate the fabric into three sections. Each section should have two strips, one of each color.

❺ Begin braiding the fabric. Cross the left section over the middle section, then the right section over the middle section. Repeat until you near the end of the fabric.

❻ Knot the end.

* Bulk fleece can be found at fabric stores.

HIDE-and-SEEK

There are a lot of different ways to play the classic game of hide-and-seek with your dog. No matter which way you play, your dog will learn along the way. Don't make it too challenging for him. You want him to be successful so that he'll play again.

Sniff, Sniff

Hide a few treats under a blanket, on a patterned rug, or in the grass. Let your dog sniff them out in his own time. When he finds the treats, he'll be so excited!

Come Find Me

Move to a different room in the house and call to your dog. Use the command "Fido, come" (page 42). When he enters the room, reward him with a treat. You may need a helper to keep your dog in place with the "Stay" command (page 46) while you hide.

Treat Puzzle

Using a muffin tin, place one treat in six of the 12 cups. Then cover all 12 cups by placing a tennis ball in each one. Now set the muffin tin on the floor. Your dog will have to sniff out the treats, then work hard to uncover them by removing the tennis balls. His efforts will be rewarded!

Dogs aren't the **only** animals that need **enrichment**. Enrichment programs are used in **zoos** with elephants, gorillas, and **sea lions**.

DIY Obstacle Course

Agility courses are used to engage your dog's mind and body. They usually involve hoops, tunnels, and more so your dog has to weave, wind, and jump his way past certain obstacles. These movements will make him agile, or able to move quickly and smoothly. In an agility course, there's a start and a finish. The trainer runs along the course with the dog, acting as a guide.

You can set up a fun course for your dog in your own backyard or at a nearby park. Teach your dog how to navigate the course by using the commands and techniques you've learned throughout this book. For example, teach him how to weave through cones by luring him through with a treat. (See the "Jump Through a Hoop" trick on page 110 for inspiration.) Once your dog begins to master the obstacle course, set a timer. See if he can improve his speed each time.

Weaving Poles

A series of at least five small disc cones (like those used in soccer or football) can act as weaving poles. They can be found at your local sporting goods store or online. Guide your dog in a zigzag motion around these obstacles.

Tunnel

A children's collapsible play tunnel, found at a toy store or online, can work for dogs too. Ideally your dog would walk through the entire tunnel on his own. Don't have a tunnel? No problem. Ask an adult for an old sheet to create a tunnel by hanging the sheet over a small table or between two chairs. Make sure it is sturdy before you start.

Dog Walk

If you're at a park, a bench can double as a balance beam, or dog walk. The goal is for your dog to jump onto it, walk along its entirety, and then jump off.

DR. GARY'S **TRAINING TIPS**

Always remember that your dog's safety comes first. Don't push him to do anything that might cause injuries. If you ever have questions about this, talk to your vet.

Tire Jump

Many agility courses require a dog to jump through a tire, but you can use a hula hoop instead. Lay a hula hoop on the ground and simply pick it up when it's time for your dog to jump through it. Turn to page 110 for tips on how to teach your dog to jump through a hoop.

Hurdle

A pool noodle rested on top of two small stacks of books makes for a great hurdle for you dog to jump over. Pool noodles are especially good because they are soft, and if the dog accidentally knocks into it, he is unlikely to get hurt.

Pause Table

A yoga mat or play mat can act as a "pause table." This is where you'll want to cue your dog to get "Down" (page 48) and hold it for five seconds.

HURDLE

HEEL

JUMP THROUGH HOOP

WEAVE

SKATEBOARDING
Pups

Skateboarding is no easy feat. It requires balance, confidence, and skill. It's certainly not a talent that every person has. But did you know that some dogs can skateboard? Hey, it helps to have four legs!

One of the most famous skateboarding dogs is Tillman, a brown-and-white English bulldog. In 2009, he became the fastest skateboarding dog while at the X Games in Los Angeles, California, U.S.A. But Tillman's fame came a couple years before that when his owner, Ron Davis, uploaded a video of his stellar skateboarding skills to the internet.

People loved watching the pup lean his body to steer the board. And when he fell off, he just hopped right back on. Sometimes Tillman would use his teeth to drag the board into place. Then he'd use his front or back paws to gain speed. There was no stopping him.

It's no surprise that the video went viral. It was seen more than 20 million times. Tillman appeared as a guest on talk shows, and his video was featured on a commercial. What a daredevil!

Bulldogs may be better at skateboarding than other dogs (and people!) because they have short, wide bodies.

HEALTHY Dog Treats

Snacks You Already Have at Home

Some human foods are OK for your dog to eat too. As long as your vet says it's OK, carry these treats with you, add them to your dog's bowl, or stuff them in a treat dispenser toy.

Apple

The nice crunch that apples provide can help clean your dog's teeth, and apples also provide a good dose of vitamins A and C. Just make sure to remove the core as well as the seeds before feeding an apple to your pup. Have an adult help you cut it up. You can serve it in thin slices or cut into small cubes. (Pears work too!)

Peanut Butter

It turns out that peanut butter is a good source of protein for both kids and dogs. Stay away from the sugar-free or "lite" versions because fake sweeteners are bad for your pup. Natural peanut butter without any added sugar is the healthiest (for you too!). If you're trying to encourage your dog to play with a certain toy, try spreading a little bit of peanut butter on top. The toy will be in his mouth before you know it!

Cheese

Thanks to its protein and calcium, cheese can be a great treat for dogs. It's high in fat though, so opt for a low-fat cheese like cottage cheese or mozzarella string cheese. Give regular-fat cheese like cheddar or Muenster only as a "once in a while" special treat.

Carrots

Carrots are a healthy low-calorie snack for you and your pup. They are high in fiber and vitamins too. Like apples, the carrot crunch is good for your dog's teeth. Try raw baby carrots or carrot sticks that are cut into bite-size pieces.

Blueberries

Low in calories and high in vitamin C and antioxidants, blueberries are a simple and easy doggy treat. After all, they're already a perfectly sized bite! You can feed your dog fresh or frozen blueberries.

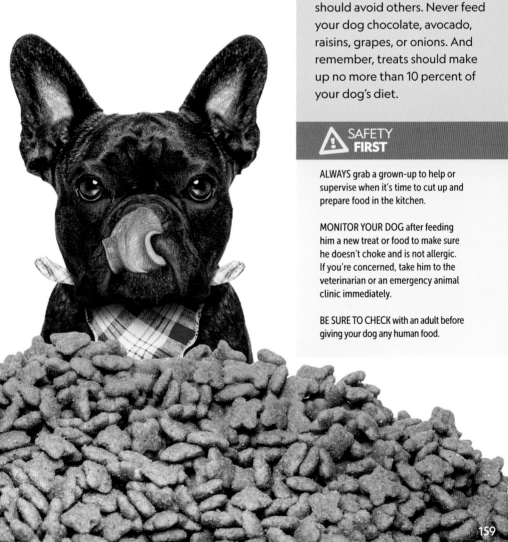

DR. GARY'S **TRAINING TIPS**

While your pup can eat some human foods, he should avoid others. Never feed your dog chocolate, avocado, raisins, grapes, or onions. And remember, treats should make up no more than 10 percent of your dog's diet.

⚠ SAFETY FIRST

ALWAYS grab a grown-up to help or supervise when it's time to cut up and prepare food in the kitchen.

MONITOR YOUR DOG after feeding him a new treat or food to make sure he doesn't choke and is not allergic. If you're concerned, take him to the veterinarian or an emergency animal clinic immediately.

BE SURE TO CHECK with an adult before giving your dog any human food.

Pet **TREAT** Bag

During the training process, you'll be giving your dog lots of treats. It's important that those rewards get to your dog at just the right time. To do that, have them in a handy bag always within reach.

You can find pre-made treat bags at pet stores and online, but perhaps you already have a small bag at home that will work. You may want to decorate it with a fabric pen or even grab a grown-up to help you sew something onto it. You can personalize it with your dog's name, a pattern, paw prints, or whatever you like.

A change purse or a pencil pouch is the perfect size for carrying small dog snacks. To make it even easier to use, attach a carabiner (found at sports or camping stores and online) through the fabric loop or key ring that's often included on these kinds of bags. Now you can easily clip it on and off your belt loop or leash handle.

A hip pack worn around your waist is also great for dog training, especially while you're on a walk. These can store treats, your clicker, and dog poop bags so you're all ready for a walk or new training session.

There are a lot of treats out there—from chewy to jerky to crunchy and flavored with things like bacon, salmon, lamb, and beef. Puppies will probably like softer treats. Talk to your veterinarian for a recommendation on which treats are best for training your dog.

Dog biscuits were invented in **1860,** but it wasn't until 1907 that an inventor named **Carleton Ellis** created dog biscuits in the **shape of a bone.**

Discover Your Dog's
FAVORITE FLAVORS

Wouldn't you love to know your dog's top treat? It's more than just an interesting fact. That knowledge could help you during the training process. Once you know your dog's snack preferences, you can save his number one choice for a "high-value reward," a treat that will really motivate your dog to listen and learn.

By placing multiple treats on the ground at the same time, your pup will hopefully slow down and consider eating the bites he likes best first. Keep track of the results and see if he has a favorite he sniffs, licks, or bites first. After you complete this test, try it again two more times (on two different days). If he goes to the same treat first each time, that's his favorite. If it's unclear, try again on different days until you get a sense of which few he likes best.

YOU NEED:

- Three sets of three different types of treats (nine treats total)
- Nine plates
- Pencil and paper

INSTRUCTIONS

1. Place one treat on each plate. Each type of treat should appear three times.
2. Place the plates on the ground in a 3 x 3 grid. That's three rows of three plates. Be sure to mix up the plates so each treat isn't grouped together.
3. Use the pencil to draw a 3 x 3 grid on a piece of paper. Label each box with the related treat.
4. Release your dog in front of the treats. Using your paper grid, record the order in which he eats the treats by numbering each box.
5. When he finishes, list the treats he selected from start to finish. Did he choose some treats over others? Were there any he wouldn't eat at all?

⚠ SAFETY FIRST

MAKE SURE that whatever you give your dog is safe for him to eat, and don't offer too many treats in one day. You need your dog to stay fit and healthy!

FURRY Film Stars

Toto, Lassie, *Air Bud* ... dogs have been starring in films since the beginning of Hollywood. That is, as long as they ace their auditions. Can you believe that dogs have auditions just like human actors would? It's true!

Once a dog is cast in a movie, a trainer guides the dog through her scenes. Trainers use commands, like the ones featured in this book, and also do a bit of acting themselves. The trainer's tone of voice and body language can have a big effect on the dog's behavior. For example, if a dog needs to look sad, the trainer will act sad by talking slowly and putting her head down low.

When dogs work on film and TV sets, the cast and crew aren't necessarily allowed to play with the animal unless they are practicing a scene together. The trainer and the handler, or wrangler as they are sometimes called, are the only ones allowed to interact with pups on set.

TOTO

Handlers make sure animals are safe and happy while they are working. They give the animals food and water, keep them out of the extreme heat or cold, make sure they are clean, and transport them safely around the set. They also make sure the animals get enough rest and exercise.

Some "movie magic" helps keep dogs safe too. Even though you see only one pooch on screen, often multiple similar-looking dogs are behind-the-scenes. Having more than one on set means that no pup will get overtired—or overfed with treats! If one is misbehaving, another one can be brought in.

If you ever see an animal get hurt in a movie, it was likely an animal substitute like a puppet or computer-generated image. Animal substitutes are helpful when stunts and costumes are involved. Rest assured that no pups are purposely injured during filming these days!

Handlers make sure animals are safe and happy while they are working.

AIR BUD

Work With Dogs
EVERY Day

Your love for dogs doesn't have to be limited to your own pet. You can work with animals in many ways when you grow up. What if every day you went to work, a pup was waiting for you!

Veterinarian

Veterinarians give checkups and tips on how best to care for pets. They also care for sick animals by treating injuries and diseases, performing surgeries, and prescribing medicine. Vets interact with animals and their owners all day. To become a veterinarian, you'll need to graduate high school, then take eight more years of schooling, at college and medical school, to receive an advanced degree in veterinary medicine.

Veterinary Technician

Veterinary technicians do the same job as human nurses, but for animals! "Vet techs" work in animal hospitals, emergency clinics, and shelters. Some vet techs specialize in one aspect of care, like surgery. They work side by side with veterinarians taking care of all kinds of animals. To become a vet tech, you'll need to graduate high school and go to school for at least two years to become certified and licensed. Veterinary assistants are like veterinary technicians but have less training and are more limited in what they can do in the clinic.

Dog Trainer

Dog trainers give owners advice on how to train their dogs. If you want to be a dog trainer, start by training your own dog. Though there is not one official school or certification for trainers, reading books on dog training and behaviors (like this one!) will help you learn a lot. Hands-on experience with real dogs is necessary. Try volunteering at your local animal shelter so you get comfortable interacting with all kinds of dogs.

Behavioral Scientist

Behavioral scientists study the actions and behaviors of humans or animals. They try to understand why humans or animals act the way they do, how they survive, and how they interact with their

environment and with others. Their findings help us understand how dogs learn and therefore the best ways to teach them. Many colleges offer degrees, even doctorates, in animal behavior.

Dog Walker

You can start your own business as a dog walker. Some dog owners need their dogs walked at least once a day while they're at work. Dog walkers go to their clients' houses, take their dog out for a walk, and return the dog—all while the owner is away. To be a successful dog walker, you must be comfortable with dogs of all breeds and sizes, as well as with picking up their poop. And you have to be OK with taking walks in the rain, wind, or cold weather.

What **KIND** of Dog Are You?

If you had fur and four legs, what kind of pup would you be? Learn how your personality compares to that of some popular dog breeds.

1. IN YOUR BEDROOM, YOU WILL FIND ...
a. tons and tons of books.
b. photos of you and your friends.
c. ribbons and trophies.

2. SOME PEOPLE MIGHT GET NERVOUS, BUT YOU DON'T MIND ...
a. memorizing a speech.
b. meeting someone new.
c. shooting a free throw in front of a crowd of people.

3. THERE'S A NEW KID IN YOUR CLASS. YOU ...
a. tell them interesting facts about your school and teacher.
b. introduce them to all of your classmates.
c. invite them to play a game of soccer at recess.

4. YOUR BEST DAY EVER WOULD INCLUDE ...
a. a stop at your favorite museum.
b. quality time with your two best friends.
c. a bike ride with your family.

5. ON THE WEEKEND, YOU CAN BE FOUND ...
a. solving a puzzle.
b. playing with friends.
c. outside, even if it's cold.

6. IT'S HARD FOR YOU TO ...
a. do nothing. You love to be busy!
b. be quiet. You love to talk!
c. sit still. You love to move!

7. YOUR FRIENDS WOULD DESCRIBE YOU AS THE ...
a. smartest person they know.
b. kindest kid in school.
c. fastest runner around.

LABRADOR RETRIEVER

BORDER COLLIE

SIBERIAN HUSKY

If you picked mostly a's, you're a …
BORDER COLLIE.

Border collies are smart, just like you! They're eager to learn and can pick up on new ideas quickly. They like to be kept busy and you do too—whether with homework, chores, or having fun with friends.

If you picked mostly b's, you're a …
LABRADOR RETRIEVER.

Labrador retrievers are known for being loyal and friendly just like you! They get along with just about anybody—both furry and human—thanks to their positive spirit. You agree that you can never have too many friends!

If you picked mostly c's, you're a …
SIBERIAN HUSKY.

Siberian huskies are athletic just like you! They're known for being fast and outgoing, and they love to work together as a team to pull a sled through the snow. When the going gets tough, Siberian huskies get going!

How Much Do You **KNOW?**

The answers to all of these questions can be found in the pages of this book. Test your knowledge to see how much you learned along the way.

1. WHEN A DOG PERFORMS A TRICK CORRECTLY, YOU SHOULD ...
a. do nothing.
b. reward him with a treat.
c. clap your hands.

2. A DOG'S BEST SENSE IS HER ABILITY TO ...
a. hear.
b. see.
c. smell.

3. WHEN A DOG SITS ON HIS REAR END WITH HIS FRONT PAWS IN THE AIR, IT'S CALLED ...
a. shaking.
b. asking for more.
c. sitting pretty.

4. DOGS LEARN BETTER WHEN YOU ...
a. reward their good behavior.
b. punish their bad behavior.
c. give them a long explanation of right and wrong.

5. WHEN YOU USE A TREAT TO GUIDE A DOG TO MOVE HER BODY A CERTAIN WAY, IT'S CALLED A ...
a. trick.
b. lure.
c. joke.

6. IF A DOG PULLS ON THE LEASH, WHAT SHOULD YOU DO?
a. Stop walking.
b. Scold him.
c. Pick him up.

Answer Key: 1. b; 2. c; 3. c; 4. a;
5. b; 6. a; 7. c; 8. c; 9. b; 10. a

7. HOW MUCH TIME SHOULD BE SPENT TRAINING YOUR DOG EACH DAY?
a. 1 hour
b. 5 minutes
c. 15 minutes

8. YOUR DOG FIDO IS IN THE BACKYARD. TO CALL FOR HIM, YOU SHOULD SAY ...
a. "Fido! Fido! Fido!"
b. "Come here, boy!"
c. "Fido, come!"

9. YOUR DOG LIKES TO JUMP ON THE COUCH EVEN THOUGH SHE'S NOT SUPPOSED TO. YOU SHOULD ...
a. throw a treat on the ground so she jumps off.
b. give the "Sit" and "Stay" cues next to the couch, then reward her with a treat.
c. yell at her until she jumps off.

10. DOGS CAN LEARN HOW MANY WORDS AND GESTURES?
a. more than 100
b. about 25
c. only a few

RESOURCES &
Further Reading

Carney, Elizabeth. *Woof! 100 Fun Facts About Dogs.* National Geographic Kids Books, 2017.

Furstinger, Nancy. *Paws of Courage: True Tales of Heroic Dogs That Protect and Serve.* National Geographic Kids Books, 2016.

Newman, Aline Alexander and Gary Weitzman. *How to Speak Dog: A Guide to Decoding Dog Language.* National Geographic Kids Books, 2013.

Quattlebaum, Mary. *Hero Dogs: True Stories of Amazing Animal Heroes!* National Geographic Kids Books, 2017.

Relser, T. J. and Gary Weitzman. *Dog Breed Guide: A Complete Reference to Your Best Friend Fur-ever.* National Geographic Kids Books, 2019.

Weitzman, Gary. *Complete Guide to Pet Health, Behavior, and Happiness.* National Geographic Books, 2019.

Wheeler-Toppen, Jodi. *Dog Science Unleashed: Fun Activities to Do With Your Canine Companion.* National Geographic Kids Books, 2018.

Websites

National Geographic Kids:
kids.nationalgeographic.com/videos/awesome-animals/#dog_genius__ep_1.mp4

kids.nationalgeographic.com/games/quizzes/quiz-whiz-dogs

kids.nationalgeographic.com/explore/photo-tips-pet-photography

kids.nationalgeographic.com/explore/books/dog-science

GLOSSARY

BEHAVIOR: The actions of a person or animal in response to its environment

BEHAVIORAL SCIENCE: The study of the actions and mannerisms of humans or animals

CHARACTERISTIC: A feature or quality that's typical of a person or animal; a trait

CUE: A hand signal or a word that represents an action

ENRICHMENT: An activity or item that stimulates an animal's senses and challenges her mind

HANDLER: The person in charge of caring for the well-being of an animal at a show or photo shoot, or on a movie or TV set; also called a wrangler

LURE: An object that attracts or draws in a person or animal

MENTAL: Relating to the brain, mind, or emotions

OBEDIENCE: Following the order or request of another

OPERANT CONDITIONING: Understanding that a learned behavior can produce a certain consequence

PHYSICAL: Relating to the body

POSITIVE REINFORCEMENT: Using rewards to encourage more of a certain type of behavior

TRAIT: A distinguishing quality of a person or animal; *see also* characteristic

UNCONDITIONED RESPONSE: A natural reaction that happens without thinking

VETERINARIAN: A doctor for animals; someone who's trained in the care and medical treatment of animals

VETERINARY TECHNICIAN: Someone who's trained to assist veterinarians in the care and medical treatment of animals

INDEX

PHOTO CREDITS

Abbreviations: GI = Getty Images; SS = Shutterstock

Cover (UP), Richard Peterson/SS; (LO), Ammit/Alamy Stock Photo; back cover: (UP), cynoclub/iStockphoto/GI; (LO), imageBROKER/Alamy Stock Photo; 2-3, Borina Olga/SS; 5, Nature Picture Library/Mark Taylor/Alamy Stock Photo; **Introduction:** 6 (BOTH), Dr. Gary Weitzman; 8 (UP LE), LightField Studios Inc./Alamy Stock Photo; 8 (UP RT), Nicky Rhodes/SS; 8 (LO), K_Thalhofer/iStockphoto/GI; 9, Megan Lorenz/iStockphoto/GI; 10-11, otsphoto/SS; 12 (LE), DEA/A. Dagli Orti/GI; 12 (RT), Boy and Dog, 'Bibius Vincit', Anguissola, Sofonisba (c.1532-1625)/Haynes Fine Art at the Bindery Galleries, Broadway/Bridgeman Images; 13 (UP), mikedabell/iStockphoto; 13 (CTR), Driving the Tandem Cart, 1905 (w/c on paper), Standing, Henry William (fl.1895-1900)/Private Collection/Wingfield Sporting Gallery, London, UK/Bridgeman Images; 13 (LO), Messenger dog in war service at the Western Front, 1917 (b/w photo)/SZ Photo/Scherl/Bridgeman Images; 14, omgimages/iStockphoto/GI; 15, imageBROKER/Gerken & Ernst/Alamy Stock Photo; 16, Steve Smith/GI; 17 (LO LE), GlobalP/iStockphoto/GI; 17 (LO RT), Utekhina Anna/SS; 17 (LO CTR RT), MirasWonderland/SS; 17 (LO CTR LE), mdmilliman/iStockphoto; 18 (UP), takayuki/SS; 18 (CTR), Life On White/Photodisc/GI; 18 (LO LE), goldenKB/iStockphoto/GI/GI; 18, jhorrocks/iStockphoto; 19 (UP), Panther Media GmbH/Alamy Stock Photo; 19 (LO), kukuruxa/SS; **Chapter 1:** 20, kali9/iStockphoto.; 22, PhotoTalk/iStockphoto; 23, s5iztok/iStockphoto/GI; 24, skynesher/iStockphoto; 25 (UP), fotyma/iStockphoto; 25 (LO), Olena Kurashova/iStockphoto; 26-27, Monkeyoum/SS; 28, TR Stok/SS; 30, Richard Peterson/SS; 31, sestovic/GI; 32, Tierfotoagentur/D. Jakob/age fotostock; 33, DenisNata/SS; 34, Dja65/SS; 35, INTERFOTO/Friedrich/Granger, NYC; 36, Quirex/GI; 39, Ariel Skelley/GI; **Chapter 2:** 40-41, SerrNovik/iStockphoto; 42, fotyma/GI; 43, Ammit/Alamy Stock PhotoAmmit; 44, Lordn/GI; 45, Eric Isselee/SS; 46, Anthony Lee/OJO Images/GI; 47, goldenKB/iStockphoto/GI/GI; 48, jhorrocks/iStockphoto; 49, Juniors Bildarchiv GmbH/Alamy Stock Photo; 50, Tierfotoagentur/D. Jakob/age fotostock; 51, Everett Collection, Inc./Alamy Stock Photo; 52, cynoclub/iStockphoto; 53, Tierfotoagentur/S. Schwerdtfeger/age fotostock; 54, PK-Photos/GI; 55, Runa Kazakova/SS; 56, blickwinkel/DuM Sheldon/Alamy Stock Photo; 57, adamkaz/GI; 58, Tierfotoagentur/J. Hutfluss/age fotostock; 59, monkeybusinessimages/iStockphoto; 60, Mint Images/GI; 61, Alena A/Dreamstime; 63 (UP), Kachalkina Veronika/SS; 63 (LO), Fertnig/GI; **Chapter 3:** 64-65, TJ_Kloster/GI; 66, Kuttig - People/Alamy Stock Photo; 67, Tobias Titz/GI; 68 (LE), Bronwyn8/Dreamstime; 68 (RT), Denis Torkhov/Dreamstime; 69, oO1shorty10o/iStockphoto; 70, Life On White/GI; 72, GlobalP/iStockphoto; 73, Frank Herholdt/GI; 74, Ivanova N/SS; 74-75, mari_art/iStockphoto; 76, Jeepsfotobox/Dreamstime; 77, blickwinkel/B. Rainer/Alamy Stock Photo; 78-79, Sian Cox/EyeEm/GI; 80, otsphoto/SS; 81, adogslifephoto/age fotostock; 82, Grigorita Ko/SS; 83, Eric Isselee/SS; 84-85, Nevena1987/iStockphoto; 86, adamelden/Stockimo/Alamy Stock Photo; 87, alexei_tm/SS; 88, Javier Brosch/SS; 89, Hillary Kladke/GI; 90, WILDLIFE GmbH/Alamy Stock Photo; 91, White House Photo/Alamy Stock Photo; 92, Chereliss/SS; 93, Hannamariah/SS; 95, Jay Christensen/Image of Sport/Newscom; **Chapter 4:** 96-97, Christian Mueller/SS; 98, dageldog/GI; 100, GlobalP/iStockphoto; 101, alexei_tm/SS; 102, pidjoe/iStockphoto; 103, Lori Jaeski/SS; 105, Jaromir Chalabala/SS; 106, Janie Airey/GI; 107, Elles Rijsdijk/EyeEm/GI; 108, PhotoMelon/GI; 109, Sarah Swinford/EyeEm/GI; 110, Daniel Reiter/STOCK4B GmbH/Alamy Stock Photo; 111, James Brey/GI; 112-113, Arterra/GI; 114-115, ZUMA Press, Inc./Alamy Stock Photo; **Chapter 5:** 116-117, Halfpoint/iStockphoto/GI; 117, cjp/GI; 118, halfmax.ru/SS; 119, Thinkstock Images/GI; 120, Gandee Vasan/GI; 122-123, CasarsaGuru/iStockphoto; 124, Peter Cade/The Image Bank/GI; 125, Paul Biris/GI; 127, Mladen Sladojevic/GI; 128, GlobalP/iStockphoto; 130, Pakorn Kumruen/EyeEm/GI; 131, Solovyova/iStockphoto; 132, mauinow1/iStockphoto; 135, Steve Cole/GI; 136, Nancy Dressel/Dreamstime; 138, Pixelrobot/Dreamstime; 139, De Meester Johan/Arterra Picture Library/Alamy Stock Photo; **Chapter 6:** 140-141, Ksenia Raykova/Dreamstime; 142-143, cynoclub/iStockphoto; 144, Przemys aw Iciak/GI; 145, SolStock/GI; 147, Zave Smith/GI; 148, Isselee/Dreamstime; 149, Mark Thiessen, NGP Staff; 150, sturti/GI; 151, alexei_tm/GI; 152, Apple Tree House/GI; 154 (LE), rhyman007/GI; 154 (RT), James Brey/GI; 154-155, Serega/iStockphoto; 155, LexiTheMonster/GI; 156, Patricia Doyle/GI; 157, Timothy A. Clary/AFP via GI; 158 (UP), Hortimages/SS; 158 (CTR), blackred/GI; 158 (LO LE), Martin Jacobs/GI; 158 (LO RT), Nattika/SS; 158-159, damedeeso/GI; 159, Anfisa Kameneva/EyeEm/GI; 160, Sbolotova/SS; 161, Zoia Lukianova/Dreamstime; 162 (dog biscuit), Spiderstock/iStockphoto; 162 (dog), Elles Rijsdijk/EyeEm/GI; 162 (plate), kyoshino/GI; 162 (treats), dlerick/GI; 163, lleerogers/iStockphoto; 164, Victor Fleming Film Company MGM/AF archive/Alamy Stock Photo; 165, Entertainment Pictures/Alamy Stock Photo; 167 (UP LE), Randy Duchaine/Alamy Stock Photo; 167 (UP RT), mezzotint_alamy/Alamy Stock Photo; 167 (LO), skynesher/GI; 168, Sharon Montrose/GI; 169 (LE), Grigorita Ko/SS; 169 (UP RT), Grigorita Ko/SS; 169 (LO RT), Stefan Cristian Cioata/GI; 170, GlobalP/iStockphoto; 171 (LE), Memitina/iStockphoto; 171 (UP RT), L.F/SS; 171 (LO RT), Olena Kurashova/SS; 172, Eric Isselee/SS; 173, 101cats/iStockphoto

To Sluggo and Zowie —Aubre Andrus

For all the heroic work of trainers and behaviorists who make the relationship with our animal companions work —Dr. Gary Weitzman

Since 1888, the National Geographic Society has funded more than 12,000 research, exploration, and preservation projects around the world. The Society receives funds from National Geographic Partners, LLC, funded in part by your purchase. A portion of the proceeds from this book supports this vital work. To learn more, visit natgeo.com/info.

NATIONAL GEOGRAPHIC and Yellow Border Design are trademarks of the National Geographic Society, used under license.

For more information, visit nationalgeographic .com, call 1-877-873-6846, or write to the following address:

National Geographic Partners
1145 17th Street N.W.
Washington, D.C. 20036-4688 U.S.A.

Visit us online at nationalgeographic.com /books

For librarians and teachers: nationalgeographic .com/books/librarians-and-teachers

More for kids from National Geographic: natgeokids.com

National Geographic Kids magazine inspires children to explore their world with fun yet educational articles on animals, science, nature, and more. Using fresh storytelling and amazing photography, *Nat Geo Kids* shows kids ages 6 to 14 the fascinating truth about the world— and why they should care.
kids.nationalgeographic.com/subscribe

For rights or permissions inquiries, please contact National Geographic Books Subsidiary Rights: bookrights@natgeo.com

Designed by James Hiscott, Jr.

National Geographic supports K–12 educators with ELA Common Core Resources. Visit natgeoed.org/commoncore for more information.

Trade paperback ISBN: 978-1-4263-3848-9
Reinforced library binding ISBN:
978-1-4263-3849-6

ACKNOWLEDGMENTS
The publisher would like to thank everyone who worked to make this book come together: Aubre Andrus and Gary Weitzman, D.V.M., writers; Priyanka Lamichhane and Libby Romero, senior editors; Erica Green, project manager; Amanda Kowalski, expert reviewer; Callie Broaddus and Brett Challos, art directors; Shannon Pallatta, design assistant; Alison Muff, photo editor; Lori Epstein, photo director; Molly Reid, production editor; and Gus Tello and Anne LeongSon, design production assistants.

Printed in China
20/RRDH/1